UNDER
THE
STARS

UNDER THE STARS

ASTROPHYSICS FOR EVERYONE

LISA HARVEY-SMITH

ILLUSTRATED BY MEL MATTHEWS

MELBOURNE
UNIVERSITY
PRESS

WS Education

Published by

WS Education, an imprint of
World Scientific Publishing Co. Pte. Ltd.
5 Toh Tuck Link, Singapore 596224
USA office: 27 Warren Street, Suite 401-402, Hackensack, NJ 07601
UK office: 57 Shelton Street, Covent Garden, London WC2H 9HE

and

Melbourne University Press
An imprint of Melbourne University Publishing Limited
Level 1, 715 Swanston Street, Carlton, Victoria 3053, Australia

National Library Board, Singapore Cataloguing in Publication Data
Name(s): Harvey-Smith, Lisa. | Matthews, Mel, illustrator.
Title: Under the stars : astrophysics for everyone / Lisa Harvey-Smith ; illustrated by Mel Matthews.
Description: Singapore : WS Education ; Carlton, Victoria : Melbourne University Press, 2020.
Identifier(s): OCN 1135729173 | ISBN 978-981-121-769-2 (hardcover) |
    978-981-121-825-5 (paperback)
Subject(s): LCSH: Astrophysics--Juvenile literature. | Cosmology--Juvenile literature. |
    Astronomy--Juvenile literature. | Universe--Juvenile literature.
Classification: DDC 523.01--dc23

British Library Cataloguing-in-Publication Data
A catalogue record for this book is available from the British Library.

Text © Lisa Harvey-Smith, 2019
Illustrations © Mel Matthews, 2019
Design and typography © Melbourne University Publishing Limited, 2019

For any available supplementary material, please visit
https://www.worldscientific.com/worldscibooks/10.1142/11756#t=suppl

Printed in Singapore

In loving memory of Tom Davies

CONTENTS

Introduction   viii

THE EARTH

Why Is the Sky Blue?   3
How Astronauts Make Shooting Stars   7
Rainbows—Nature's Lightshow   11
Starry Starry Night   15
Where Does Space Begin?   19
Why the Wind Blows   23
The Upside-Down World of Telescopes   27
The Wonky Reason for Seasons   31
Constellations—Shapes in the Stars   35
Counting Down to a Launch   39
The People Who Study Outer Space   43
How Your Eyes Make Stargazing Extraordinary   45
The Problem of Space Junk   49
The Ever-Spinning Earth   53
Comets—The Hairy Stars of Doom   55
Gravity Keeps Us Grounded   59
Life on a Space Station   61
Stopping Cosmic Rays   65
Real Rocket Science   69

THE SOLAR SYSTEM

Our Very Own Star   75
Mercury—The Planet that Hugs the Sun   79
Venus—Cloudy with a Chance of Acid   83

The Earth and the Sun—The Best of Friends   87
Seeing Red on Mars   91
How Jupiter Got Its Stripes   95
Saturn Has a Nice Ring to It   99
Uranus Is Full of Gas   103
Neptune—The Unseen Planet   107
The Dark World of Pluto   111
Asteroid Belts and Icy Clouds   113
How Much Would You Weigh on Other Planets?   117
The Secret Life of the Sun   121

EXTRASOLAR SPACE

Pulsars—The Incredible Spinning Stars   127
Is There Life on Other Planets?   131
A Guide to Spotting Exoplanets   135
Supernova! When Stars Explode   139
The Biggest Star in the Sky   143
How Does a Star Become a Black Hole?   147

THE MILKY WAY

Our Galaxy—Countless Stars   153
Supermassive—Visiting a Black Hole   157

THE UNIVERSE

Travelling at the Speed of Light   163
Why Do Quasars Shine So Bright?   167
The Big Bang Theory   171
Surfing Gravitational Waves   175
How Big Is the Universe?   177

Further Exploring   180
Acknowledgements   181

INTRODUCTION

I was six years old when I first looked up at the night sky with my dad. We were searching for Halley's comet, a celestial visitor that appears in our sky only once every seventy-six years. We didn't manage to see the comet—it was very faint and the sky was quite cloudy. But investigating this secretive world and contemplating the stars for the first time opened up a universe that I had never imagined. My dreams soared.

Looking at the sky and asking 'Why?' led me into a fascinating hobby: astronomy, the science of the stars. My mum took me along to a local astronomy club and I learned so much from the other members and guest speakers. I borrowed the club's telescope and spent my evenings studying the craters on the moon and tracing the Orion nebula, a glowing region of gas more than 1000 light-years away where new stars are being created.

Now, as a professional astronomer, I still love contemplating the mysteries of the universe and using scientific methods to learn more. Using science, in particular physics, to study the universe and understand more about it is called astrophysics. In my job, I have used some of the largest, most powerful telescopes in the world, and ones that orbit the Earth too. I've travelled to deserts, mountains and jungles in my search for the best close-up views of the night sky. I've zoomed into the birth and death of stars. I've weighed black holes in distant galaxies. As a scientist, I have seen things that no-one has ever seen before.

Under the Stars: Astrophysics for Everyone might make your own dreams soar. I hope that you enjoy learning about our amazing universe. There are some useful links listed at the end of this book so that you can explore more for yourself.

Think big and enjoy the journey.

Lisa

PART 1

THE EARTH

WHY IS THE SKY BLUE?

The light from our nearest star, the Sun, constantly floods the Earth. This intense glow comes from the unimaginably hot middle of the Sun, which is burning at the extraordinarily high temperature of 15 million degrees Celsius. Since the Earth is round, the Sun shines steadily down on half of our world at any one time—so when the Sun is in the sky above one-half of the planet, it is daytime there, while the other half sleeps in darkness.

The Sun is, on average, around 150 million kilometres from the Earth. Sunlight travels all that way through deep space to reach us. Each beam of light takes eight minutes to complete this incredible journey. When the light reaches the Earth, it first passes through our atmosphere, a thick layer of air that reaches 80 kilometres into the sky. The atmosphere acts as a protective blanket for our planet.

It keeps us warm, it stops space rocks from hitting our heads, and of course, it provides the air that we need to breathe in order to stay alive.

Our atmosphere is made up of molecules, the microscopic building blocks of, well, everything. Many of the molecules in our atmosphere are made up of chemicals like nitrogen and oxygen. Since light waves are so small, they bounce off these molecules. The air molecules act like millions of tiny mirrors, reflecting this light.

Sunlight is made up of all the colours of the rainbow. You can see these hidden colours if you let sunlight shine through a crystal or a prism. If you are lucky, you will see tiny rainbows sprinkled around the room. The way in which sunlight bounces off molecules of air depends on the colour of the light.

Red light waves are stretched out, so that when they interact with the molecule 'mirrors', the red colours are hardly scattered at all. But blue colours travel in a slightly different way. They move in tight bundles, bouncing off the molecules randomly and scattering in all directions. That's why our sky is blue.

Not all planets have blue skies. The colour depends on the make-up of the atmosphere. On the Moon, the sky is black, even in the daytime. That's because there is no atmosphere on the Moon. There are no tiny mirrors to reflect the light. The sky on Mars is very different. It's red! That's because Mars has a very thin atmosphere compared with the Earth's, with hardly any molecules in it. There are hardly any tiny mirrors and so there is very little scattered blue light.

Mars also has a lot of red dust in its sky. If you were standing on the surface of the planet, it would seem like you were in the middle of a huge dust storm most of the time. And this dust absorbs blue light better than red light.

Light and colour are amazing! Next time you look up at the beautiful blue sky, think about the incredible journey that light has taken from the Sun.

HOW ASTRONAUTS MAKE SHOOTING STARS

Have you ever looked up at the night sky and seen a shooting star? Maybe you made a wish.

Shooting stars are not stars at all. They just look like stars. They are actually tiny space adventurers—pieces of space dust—that wander too close to the Earth. When they crash into the layer of air around our planet—the atmosphere—they burn up, creating a very bright streak of light. Another name for a shooting star is a meteor.

Meteors can appear at any time. You can see them any night of the week, as long as the sky is dark. If you go somewhere that's well away from city lights, such as a park, the beach or out in the country, and look patiently at the sky for half an hour, you're quite likely to see one. They can fall from any direction.

Shooting stars also come in groups. A few times every year we can predict exactly when and where a shower of shooting stars will appear.

We see so many meteors because space is full of dust. It's not like the dust in your house. Rather, it's tiny specks of rock and dirt that never became part of planets and moons. In your home, you can use a vacuum cleaner to suck up dust. In space, our planet acts as a vacuum cleaner, sucking up the dust as it swooshes around the Sun.

When a tiny speck of space dust falls towards the Earth, it leaves the darkness of outer space and enters the atmosphere. As it falls, it rubs against the air. To find out what happens to the dust, rub your hands together really fast for ten seconds. What happened? That's right—friction made your hands very hot.

The same thing happens to the space dust as it flies through the atmosphere. As it gathers speed, hurtling towards the ground at 50 kilometres per second, the temperature of a tiny speck of dust can reach more than 1000 degrees Celsius. In a few short seconds, it burns up completely—nothing is left. We call this amazing spectacle a meteor, or a shooting star.

Meteor showers happen when the Earth's orbit crosses a lane of space dust left in the wake of a comet. You can see hundreds of shooting stars every hour! It's a great thing to watch.

While most shooting stars are made from natural space dust, a very small number are made by objects that humans have launched into space and that have later fallen back to Earth. They might be pieces of spacecraft that are no longer needed in orbit. Or they can be more personal in nature.

You see, when astronauts go to the toilet in space, there is no water pipe to take their waste away. Instead, astronauts such as those on the International Space Station jettison their poo into space. This poo is fired quickly towards the Earth and burns up in the atmosphere. Just like a shooting star.

The next time you see a meteor, make a wish. Try this one: 'I hope that astronaut poo doesn't fall on my head!'

RAINBOWS—NATURE'S LIGHTSHOW

Have you ever seen a rainbow? I'll bet you have. These giant arches of light are amazing. They are nature's beautiful lightshow.

Rainbows reach across the sky, as far as you can see. Their glowing light is separated into thin bands of colour—red, orange, yellow, green, blue, indigo and violet light. Rainbows are very special because we don't see them often. They only happen when it's sunny and rainy at the same time.

Imagine that it's a bright and glorious day with no clouds in the sky. No rainbows here—you need rain to make a rainbow. Now the weather changes and a few dark clouds pass by. A short rain shower begins. Between the clouds, a sunny spell dries everything up. Now this is more like it. These are prime viewing conditions for rainbows.

How is a rainbow formed? A rainbow appears when sunshine bounces off raindrops. The sunlight shines on the front of a raindrop, travels all the way through the water, then bounces off the back of the raindrop, which is like a mirror. The light then goes back out the front of the raindrop and towards your eyes.

As the light from the Sun passes through a raindrop, it gets spread out into many different colours. That's because some colours of light are bent more than others as they travel through water. Violet light is bent the most, so we see this colour on the inside of the rainbow. Red is bent the least—we see this on the outside of the rainbow. You end up seeing a giant arc of light layered in its many amazing colours.

We only ever see rainbows directly opposite the Sun. The line between you and the Sun will be at the exact centre of the rainbow. If you and a friend both look at a rainbow while standing side-by-side, you will actually see two completely different rainbows!

Rainbows are most common in the morning and the evening. This is when the Sun is low in the sky, which means the rainbow will be high in the sky. We also see rainbows in other places. Have you ever turned on a hose on a sunny day? You can sometimes see the colours of a rainbow in the fine mist of water. And when you visit a waterfall, you might be lucky enough to see a small rainbow in the water spraying into the air.

We can even see rainbows around the Moon. On a very cold night, crystals of ice hang high up in the Earth's atmosphere.

These reflect light, creating a faint rainbow all the way around the Moon—we call these Moon-bows, or haloes.

Next time you see a rainbow, just imagine how the sunlight is bouncing off millions of tiny raindrops and spreading out into all of its magnificent colours!

STARRY STARRY NIGHT

During the day, the sky is very bright. That's because the Sun is above our heads and its light is shining down on us. The Sun's light is scattered off molecules in the air and makes the sky appear blue.

Without the Sun, we would have no daylight at all. That means plants would not grow and animals would have no food. The Earth would become completely cold and dark. Life on our planet would end. We are very lucky to have our star shining down on us every day.

When it is night-time, the part of the Earth where you live has spun away from the Sun. The Sun is shining on the other side of the Earth and the sunlight cannot reach you, which is why it is dark.

The night doesn't last forever. The world turns one complete revolution every day—the Sun rises again as your side of the planet rotates towards it, and the cycle continues. But in some parts of the world, near the north or south poles, it is dark all the time in winter and light all the time in summer. Can you imagine living in such a place?

Although we are daytime mammals, the night-time is still important to humans. We use it to sleep and rest, which keeps us healthy and mentally alert. Many animals, such as birds, kangaroos, wombats, owls and flying foxes, use the safety of the darkness to hunt and collect food.

The night sky, however, is not completely dark.

The Moon sometimes shines at night. The light from the Sun travels all the way to the Moon and bounces off its surface as if it was a mirror, landing in our eyes and brightening up the night. Without the light from the Sun, the Moon would be invisible to us.

The planets also shine in our night sky. But these also rely on the light from the Sun. The planets act as reflectors of the Sun's light, and without that light, they would also disappear from our view.

There are other sources of light in the universe apart from the Sun, the Moon and the planets. Can you guess what they are? That's right, the stars. There are more than 1 billion trillion stars in the universe that we could possibly see from Earth. These stars all shine just as brightly as the Sun. They only seem fainter because they are so far away.

But if the night sky is filled with stars, why is it dark?

There are two reasons for this. Firstly, there is a lot of space dust out there, which blocks much of the light from distant stars. And secondly, because the stars are so far away, and because they are whooshing away from us as the universe expands, their light has been diluted. Light from VERY far away turns invisible as its waves stretch through the expanding universe.

As you can see, day and night are not always as simple as they seem.

WHERE DOES SPACE BEGIN?

Our amazing planet is surrounded by a beautiful thin layer of blue atmosphere. The Earth's air is a complex mix of 78 per cent nitrogen, 21 per cent oxygen, and many other gases in much smaller amounts. At ground level, the air is thick and plentiful, more than enough for us to breathe. And since we need a constant supply of oxygen for our muscles and brains to work, getting enough air is pretty important. But as we go higher up, the atmosphere becomes much thinner, and in each lungful of air there is less nitrogen, less oxygen and less of the other gases.

The highest mountain in the world is Mount Everest. It is 8.8 kilometres high. On the top of Everest, the air is so thin that it is very hard to breathe. People who climb this mountain often take oxygen tanks along to help them survive. Without this equipment, high up on the mountain, climbers can barely take two steps before having to stop for a rest.

Aeroplanes can fly even higher than Mount Everest. People can breathe comfortably inside planes because the cabins are pressurised. That means more air is pumped into the aeroplane from the outside to keep the air pressure steady as the plane climbs higher. There is plenty of oxygen inside the cabin, but if we ventured outside the plane we would quickly die.

As we go up into our atmosphere, even higher than an aeroplane, the air gets gradually thinner until there is almost none left. Where the atmosphere ends, outer space begins. The sky goes completely black, since there are no molecules of air there to scatter the sunlight.

We define the edge of space as being 100 kilometres above sea level—although space really has no definite edge, just a gradual boundary. Above this, there is hardly any air at all. If you fly more than 100 kilometres above the Earth, you are officially an astronaut. When you become an astronaut, you will receive a special badge called 'astronaut wings'. More than 500 people have travelled into space since the first human spaceflight in 1961.

A pure vacuum is a place that has no atoms or particles in it—it is completely, 100 per cent empty. But outer space is not totally empty. There are still some things floating out there. For instance, there are tiny, subatomic particles called cosmic rays all over the place. And of course, there are meteors and comets and planets and gas clouds and stars as well.

The view of Earth from space is incredibly beautiful. The atmosphere looks like a thin, blue, fuzzy layer. The clouds are white and fluffy. The oceans glisten and dazzle in the sunlight. Continents appear red, brown and green, depending on the colour of the soil and the amount of vegetation. Mountains crinkle between the flat plains.

No countries or boundaries can be seen, just one big beautiful Earth. Our home.

WHY THE WIND BLOWS

We've all been outside on a windy day. Treetops can sway like dancers, with some birds holding on for dear life through the gusts and squalls. Braver birds soar, circling high above our heads on a buoyant carpet of air. Clouds skip across the sky like light-footed skinks. Paddocks are filled with the crackling of thousands of rushes. White-lipped waves smash on ocean cliffs, turning into a drizzly spray. Rain is driven sideways.

Have you ever wondered what makes the wind blow? It all depends on the air's temperature.

As sunlight falls onto the Earth, it warms our planet's surface. Different parts of the Earth receive different amounts of sunlight, so some areas take up more heat than others. For example, the land heats up quickly during the day and cools down quickly at night. The sea, on the other hand, takes longer to warm up in the morning, but it holds onto its heat at night. This means different parts of the Earth's surface have different temperatures.

The heat from the ground slowly warms up the surrounding air. When air gets warm, it expands and becomes lighter. And as the cooler, heavier air around it sinks, this warm air rises. It's a bit like a helium balloon floating above the atmosphere. When the warm air rises, it is replaced by cooler air from its surroundings. This process creates a current of air.

These currents can also form near mountains or valleys. Because its path is blocked, the air is pushed out of the way by these enormous geographical features.

Wind can be very powerful. Sometimes, in the region near the equator called the tropics, circulations of air called cyclones can form. These have very strong winds—they blow up to 200 kilometres per hour—that can push over cars, aeroplanes and buildings.

On a much smaller scale, within thunderstorms, very powerful circulations of air called tornadoes can whip up winds of up to 300 kilometres per hour. Tornadoes form in rotating clouds called supercells, which are dragged towards the ground when very heavy rain pulls the base of the cloud towards the Earth.

On a typical day, rather than an extreme one, we can harness the power of the wind. Using wind turbines, we can generate clean and sustainable electricity—no fossil fuels involved. This is very good for our planet.

Weather scientists are called meteorologists. They use instruments such as a special windmill called an anemometer (not an anteater; an *an-em-om-eater*), which spins around and measures how fast the wind is blowing.

High up in the atmosphere, meteorologists can measure the speed of the wind using a weather balloon filled with helium. By tracking the motion of the balloon over a period of several hours or even days, we can figure out where the wind is blowing high up and how fast it is going. This helps us to plan the fastest and most efficient routes for aeroplanes to fly between continents.

Science has shown us that the wind is air moving from one place to the next due to different temperatures around the planet. It is the endless, ceaseless wind.

THE UPSIDE-DOWN WORLD OF TELESCOPES

One of the best tools we have ever invented for looking at the stars is the telescope.

Telescopes do two clever things. Firstly, they make things look bigger and closer than they really are. By bending light through a big piece of glass called a lens, the image of an object is stretched and the object itself seems much bigger. That means we can see more detail, whether it's the craters on the Moon, the make-up of a cluster of stars, or the spiralling arms of a distant galaxy.

The way in which light is bent by a telescope's lens also makes the image flip upside-down. So everything you see in a telescope is the wrong way up! It doesn't really matter, though, because there is no up and down in space. Plus you can always turn the image upside-down.

Telescopes also make things look brighter. Because telescopes are bigger than our eyes, they collect more light, which means that you end up with a brighter picture. Using a telescope, then, we can see very faint stars that are incredibly far away.

The first telescopes were invented more than 400 years ago. On a quiet day in his workshop, a Dutch optician called Hans was playing with some spectacle lenses. He noticed that if he held two lenses apart and looked through them both at the same time, he could make faraway things look closer. Clever or what?

Hans wrote down this idea and published it, and soon others began to use this invention to look at the Moon and the stars and the planets. The study of the universe with telescopes was a very significant breakthrough that has helped us to understand so much more about the Moon, our solar system and even gravity.

We now have many different types of telescopes. Some look at light like our eyes do. Others look at the invisible colours of light, like radio waves, infra-red and X-rays. By looking at these invisible colours, we have discovered many exciting things, like black holes ripping stars to pieces!

You won't find many big telescopes in cities. That's because streetlights wash out our view of the stars. We call this light pollution and it is a big challenge for astronomers. There are so many people in the world and so many streetlights for them that there are hardly any dark places left for studying the night sky. The problem is that many streetlights don't just shine light towards the ground, where it is needed. They also shine light up into the sky, where it is not needed.

The sky over big telescopes is often protected by law from light pollution. People who live near these telescopes put shields on top of their streetlights to stop the light from illuminating the sky. If we all did this, the night sky would look amazing everywhere and less energy would be wasted. Wouldn't that be a good thing?

Another challenge for astronomers is the Earth's atmosphere. The air in our atmosphere moves around a lot and there are pockets of air at different temperatures. This makes starlight bounce around the sky. It's why the stars twinkle. Now, the twinkling of stars makes for a nice nursery rhyme, but it doesn't help us to study them. If the image of a star is dancing all over the place, we can't get a clear view.

To avoid this, many of our largest telescopes are built ABOVE the atmosphere, such as on a very high volcano or mountaintop. Some are even built in space. The Hubble Space Telescope is the most famous of these. It has taken thousands of incredible pictures of stars, galaxies and nebulae (patches of interstellar dust and gas), all of which you can download for free on the internet. Space telescopes are hugely expensive to build, but they really do take the best pictures.

If you want to get a good view of the stars, you don't need to fly into space. With a small telescope, you can see the craters on the Moon, the rings of Saturn, and Jupiter's four biggest moons. It's a worthwhile pocket-money project!

THE WONKY REASON
FOR SEASONS

Imagine that it's twenty years into the future and you're now an astronaut. You climb into your rocket, blast off from the Earth, whoosh past the Moon and the planets, and get set to leave our solar system. If you look back towards our home, what do you see?

There is the Sun at the centre of the solar system, shining steadily. And there are the eight planets, all orbiting the Sun in the same direction. Then you notice that the planets don't circle the Sun randomly. They all lie in a single line, flat as a pancake, which we call the ecliptic.

Many of the planets spin on their axes in the same direction as their orbits around the Sun. But some, including the Earth, are different. The Earth's poles are wonky, bent over at an angle of 23.5 degrees from upright. We don't know for sure why the Earth spins at an angle, but we think it might have been involved in a crash with another planet early in its life.

What does all this have to do with the seasons?

Because the Earth's poles are wonky, as the planet orbits the Sun once every year, the angle of the poles changes relative to the Sun. In December, the South Pole points towards the Sun. That means that the southern half of the Earth—the Southern Hemisphere—gets more sunlight than the northern half.

At this time in the south, it is hotter and we enjoy our summer. In December at the South Pole, it is sunny all the time—even at night! It must be really hard to sleep with no night-time. Despite this, around 200 people live at the South Pole research station in the summer months.

But slowly, the Earth keeps orbiting the Sun. Come March, the north and south poles are edge-on to the sun. Autumn begins in the south and the weather cools. Trees begin to change colour and drop their leaves. Every part of the Earth gets an equal amount of daylight.

The Earth continues on. In June, the South Pole is pointed away from the Sun. The northern half of the planet takes the bulk of the sunlight, so it is winter in the Southern Hemisphere.

At the South Pole in June it is completely dark—the sun never rises. Only about fifty hardy scientists and technicians live at the research station then. They have to be careful with all their food and medical supplies, as no aircraft can land because of the harsh weather.

For most of the Southern Hemisphere, the Sun sets early and the evenings are dark. It's also dark when we wake up in the morning, since the Sun is too busy shining down on the Northern Hemisphere to come and visit us for long.

But the Earth again moves on. Once it is September, the poles move back to their edge-on position relative to the Sun. Spring is upon us in the south. The weather warms again and leaves grow from the trees.

Like our journey around the Sun, the cycle of seasons is never-ending.

CONSTELLATIONS–SHAPES IN THE STARS

Have you ever been outside at night somewhere really dark and looked at the stars? Have you watched them twinkle and shine, cascading across the heavens as if they are performing for you? Have you caught sight of the Southern Cross? Or the saucepan? Or the emu?

The stars can be breathtaking. Some are dazzling white jewels, some are a piercing blue, and some glow steadily with pale orange light. With their different colours, brightness and patterns, the stars are laid out across the sky like a beautiful tapestry.

For thousands of years we have tried to make sense of the stars. People have made up names for the patterns above us and created stories to explain how they got there. The oldest written star maps are more than 3000 years old, while those that have been passed down through cultural stories and songs may be even older.

There are stories of magical animals that live in the sky, like the great bear, the scorpion and the crab. There are tales of ancient sky gods, like Orion and the seven sisters. We even see shapes in the stars that look like everyday objects, like microscopes. These are all constellations.

A constellation is a shape that we imagine in the stars. What we see are not really saucepans or crabs or bears, of course. They are just beaming balls of gas. It's just that there are so many stars spread across our magnificent night sky that when it's really dark, away from city lights, we can imagine another world up there, filled with fantastic creatures.

The stories have varied greatly in different parts of the world. Europeans and Middle Eastern peoples saw gods in the sky and linked the constellations to complicated tales of morality. In South America, there were stories of llamas and frogs, while the ancient Chinese saw dragons and tortoises. Native Americans saw bison and bears. Aboriginal and Torres Strait Islander peoples talk of an emu in the sky, its position telling them when to gather emu eggs.

These are all important historical stories because they told our ancestors how to live, navigate and gather food. Polynesians used the stars to make incredible navigational charts, which enabled them to find their way between hundreds of islands from Hawaii to New Zealand. Europeans used star charts for centuries to navigate the world in big ships. Naval officers and astronauts still learn how to use the stars as a navigational tool, just in case modern arrangements like the global positioning system (GPS) fail.

The constellations will not last forever. Because stars are moving through space, their positions in the sky will move too. In a few thousand years, the shapes of animals and sky gods (and saucepans!) will have dissolved. Maybe the people who are alive then will make up new constellations

You can find pictures of the constellations on a star map or through a star-finding app. It's great fun to look for the constellations, even to challenge yourself to find them all. You might also enjoy inventing your own constellations. They could be starry shapes that look like your favourite toys, pets, even your friends and family. Next time you go out at night, why not draw a star map and give this a try.

COUNTING DOWN TO
A LAUNCH

The day you have been waiting for your whole life has finally
arrived.

Since you were selected to be an astronaut three years ago,
you have been completely focused on your goal and trained
hard every day. Together with your crewmates, you have practised
using the controls and procedures of your spacecraft thousands of
times. As part of your training, you floated in microgravity on a
special aircraft that flew high into the atmosphere and then dived
downwards, leaving you weightless for a few moments. You even
designed the scientific experiments that you will carry out on the
International Space Station.

You know you are ready. Looking at your reflection in the
bathroom mirror, you realise that what you have been working for
is now at hand.

In the small but spotless quarantine quarters, you carefully prepare for the task ahead. At your final breakfast on Earth before the mission, you and your crewmates eat quietly and thoughtfully, preparing for the serious business that's about to unfold. You brush your teeth and read the notes that your family has prepared, wishing you luck and telling you they love you. At 8.24 a.m. precisely, the ground mission crew knock on your door. Time to go, they say.

You and your two crewmates, dressed in heavy spacesuits and holding helmets, climb into a white car. The vehicle drives slowly along an otherwise empty road towards the towering rocket standing proud on Launch Pad 1. With butterflies in your stomach, you climb out of the car and pose for a final photograph with the crew under the intimidating rocket, which is as high as a skyscraper and is coming alive with the fuel needed to propel its payload into space.

You walk through a metal door into a dark corridor and wait impatiently for a lift to take you to the top of this enormous structure. Your eyes grow wide as they adjust to the dark, and you begin to imagine everything that will happen in the next few hours, and in the days ahead. You step into the lift, which speeds upwards and comes to a halt at the sixteenth floor, which provides access to the crew module.

Striding now with a sense of purpose, you arrive at the final metal door. The ground crew open the hatch. You survey the inside of the module, so familiar from your months of training. It is a small space with three seats that face upwards towards your destination and also a control console covered by hundreds of buttons and switches.

Finally, you squeeze into the centre seat, with your head reclining backwards and your body facing up, towards the sky. The hatch closes and you wait. After what seems like an eternity, the countdown begins.

Ten ... nine ... eight ... your hands grip the seat ... seven ... six ... five .... four ... three ... you shut your eyes tight ...

THE PEOPLE WHO STUDY
OUTER SPACE

Some scientists study the weather, or plants, or polar bears. Others invent new chemicals, cure diseases, or figure out how the human brain works. Astronomers study outer space.

We try to understand what's above the clouds and beyond the Moon. We build gigantic telescopes that help us to see things that are invisible to our eyes. These aren't like the ones you might use in your garden at home. These are HUUUUUGGGE telescopes on mountaintops, in deserts, even in space.

We watch stars explode in distant galaxies. We look in amazement as planets and moons skip around our solar system. We study stars to make sense of how they live and die. We measure the size of black holes in galaxies millions of light-years away and try to figure out how they behave.

Being an astronomer is an amazing job because sometimes you get to see something no-one has EVER seen before. That feels pretty special. Would you like to be an astronomer?

HOW YOUR EYES MAKE STARGAZING EXTRAORDINARY

Eyes are truly incredible. Most creatures have them, and they have evolved over more than 500 million years to adapt to different tasks.

Some animals can see colours that are invisible to humans. The dragonfly is one. It has more than 30 000 sensors on each of its eyes which can detect ultraviolet and polarised light. Mantis shrimp have astonishing eyes that can see twelve colours, plus ultraviolet and infra-red, that humans can't see at all! Then there are chameleons, which have two eyes that can move independently of one another. This means they can spot potential food (or danger) in any direction.

Human eyes are pretty amazing too. Did you know that we have in-built sunglasses that adapt to the light and help us see in the dark?

If you go outdoors during the day, when the sky is filled with sunlight, the little black circles at the front of your eyes, called pupils, become quite small. Your pupils shrink in bright sunlight to prevent your eyes from receiving too much heat, light and ultraviolet rays, which could damage your vision. When you step inside again, the light level is now lower and your pupils expand to let more light in—slowly, your eyes adjust until you can see much better.

You can do some experiments with a friend at home to see how pupils work. Firstly, go indoors with your friend and look into their eyes to see how big their pupils are. Now turn on a light and have your friend look towards it. Can you see their pupils shrink? When they look away, the pupils will slowly grow again. (Just a reminder—never, ever look directly at the Sun as it will permanently damage your eyesight.)

Your amazing stretching pupils also help you see in the dark.

When it's night-time, try turning off all the lights in your house and opening your curtains. Can you see any stars? How many? Now leave the lights off for a few more minutes and then look out at the stars again. Do you notice anything different?

At night, your eyes slowly start to trust the darkness and your pupils open up very wide. Chemical changes also happen in the retina at the back of your eye, switching off your colour receptors and turning up the volume on your black-and-white vision. Since your black-and-white vision is much more powerful than your colour vision, these changes make your eyes far more sensitive to light.

Believe it or not, if you sit in the dark for about thirty minutes, your eyes will become up to a million times more sensitive than they are in bright sunlight. This allows the stars to look much brighter and more magnificent.

Many animals have even better night vision than us. That's because they have many more light receptors at the back of their eyes. Animals that hunt at night also have a special mirror at the back of their eyes that reflects light back through their retinas.

Aren't eyes extraordinary?

THE PROBLEM OF
SPACE JUNK

Space junk is the term for litter that humans have dropped in space. We're not talking about lolly wrappers and plastic bottles though. This is stuff like discarded rocket boosters, unused satellites, and even flecks of paint that have peeled off the outside of a spacecraft and then float aimlessly in Earth's orbit.

Before the middle of the last century, humans had never sent anything into space. The only thing orbiting the Earth was the Moon and a few bits of rock. But in 1957, the Soviet Union—now Russia—launched the Sputnik 1 satellite and changed the world forever.

Today there are around 1500 human-made satellites in space. These range in size from a shoebox to a house! These satellites do very important things, like beaming live TV signals around the world, studying the weather and climate of Earth, and making the location services and maps in our mobile devices work. Without these satellites, we wouldn't have the global positioning system (GPS).

Normally, when we are finished with a satellite, a small rocket booster fires it gently down towards the Earth and it burns up safely in the atmosphere on the way. It's like putting a lolly wrapper in the bin. But not all spacecraft are disposed of this responsibly, and there have been accidents. In 2009, two satellites collided at high speed over Siberia. The debris from that collision still orbits the Earth today, posing a real risk to satellites and astronauts.

There are now more than 129 million pieces of space junk orbiting the Earth. Most of them are smaller than your little fingernail.

You might be wondering, if space junk is that small, why is it a problem? Well, even small pieces of space junk can do enormous damage to a spacecraft. That's because they are travelling at immense speeds. When a piece of metal hits a spacecraft at several kilometres per second, it can blast right through the outer skin, knock the spacecraft off course, or destroy the solar panels that power the vehicle. Satellites worth tens of millions of dollars have been destroyed by such impacts.

Most spacecraft now have a special bumper, called a Whipple shield, to give them some protection from these collisions. Spacecraft can also perform orbital manoeuvres to quickly get out of the way of any debris.

Space junk is clearly hazardous to human life, with astronauts living and working in Earth's orbit. Fortunately, we know where a lot of the larger fragments are because we track them with special telescopes. This allows us to warn the astronauts on the International Space Station of approaching debris, and if necessary they can evacuate to a special capsule that will keep them safe.

There are various plans to get rid of space junk, but it is not easy. The ideas include using special robots to pick up the junk and drag it out of orbit, and putting fishing nets in space to snag this high-speed litter. But neither of these options has yet been seriously tested due to their high costs.

If you were to design a system to get rid of space junk, what would it look like?

THE EVER-SPINNING EARTH

Dawn is coming. As the sky brightens in the east, a creeping blue lightens the horizon, becoming a watercolour blue that leaks into the sky. At the same time, a dazzling star fades. Birds begin to cheep and crow, part of the dawn choir that heralds the new day.

The Sun peeks over the horizon, its light hazy and red as it yawns and then jostles through the atmosphere. Losing its blue colours along the way, the light is scattered by the air, painting the eastern sky with an orange tinge.

As our planet spins on, slowly but surely the Sun moves higher above our heads. The sky shines confidently, deep and rich, with a radiant blue.

Morning wears on. The Earth keeps turning and we spin away from the Sun. Eventually, in the late afternoon, its bright yellow glow dips towards the west, softening the blue. Tinges of purple and orange kiss the clouds as the last rays of light beam down from a dusky sky.

The Earth spins onwards.

COMETS–THE HAIRY STARS OF DOOM

A long time ago, before humans invented telescopes, there was a lot about the night sky we didn't understand. Back then, people were very superstitious. They were scared of the unknown and believed all sorts of fantastical stories about the stars.

Once in a lifetime, a bright new object would come into the sky and move slowly between the stars every night. Sometimes the object would grow a long head of hair that trailed behind it as it swooped around the Sun. These were called hairy stars, or comets (from the Greek word *kometes*, which means 'long-haired').

The strange and sudden appearance of comets made people even more scared. Many believed they brought individuals bad luck, or caused natural disasters.

They don't, of course. Comets are actually quite harmless little things—provided they don't crash into us. They are dirty snowballs made of rock and ice that fly around the solar system.

Unlike the planets in our solar system, which travel in fairly circular orbits, comets go REALLY far away from the Sun and then come REALLY close to it, following an egg-shaped orbit. When they are far away, we can't see them at all because they are small—most of them are the size of a regular country town—and they only shine by the light reflected from the Sun. But when they get close to the Sun, it's a different story altogether.

The heat from the Sun warms the comet up and the ice on its surface begins to melt. As it gets hotter still, the comet steams like a kettle, creating an atmosphere called a coma (*co-ma*). Light and particles from the Sun start to crash into that coma and push it back, away from the Sun, to form a tail. A comet's tail can be a million kilometres long—that's three times longer than the distance from the Earth to the Moon!

Its journey close to the Sun sees the comet become big and bright in our night sky. Sunlight reflects off its new cloak of vapour and its enormous tail, providing a fascinating beacon in the sky for us to observe. Once the comet gets further away from the Sun, its tail starts to dissolve—its 'hair' falls out. The cloud of vapour cools down and is replaced by ice once again. The comet then goes back into hibernation as a dirty snowball.

Halley's comet takes seventy-six years to do one revolution around the Sun. As it orbits our solar system, it is only visible for a few weeks at a time, when it gets very close to the Earth and the Sun—although humans have been noticing it for thousands of years. The last time it was visible from Earth, in 1986, the European Space Agency sent a spacecraft to fly past and take a closer look. The adults in your family might have looked up at night and seen the comet as a fuzzy 'star' with a long mane of hair.

Halley's comet won't return until the year 2061. How old will you be then? Do you think you might see Halley's comet?

GRAVITY KEEPS US GROUNDED

Imagine jumping into the air, as high as you possibly can. But however hard you try, you land back on the ground with a bump. What is stopping you from jumping higher? Why can't you leap above the trees, spring far above the clouds, soar even higher than the Moon? It's because gravity is keeping you on the Earth.

Gravity is a force, of course. It's an invisible pull between the Earth and you. It keeps us on the ground. But gravity works in space too. It is gravity that makes the Earth orbit the Sun, once every year. It's gravity that binds the Earth and the Moon together in a never-ending dance.

Imagine if there was no gravity at all. What would happen to us? We'd start to float away, high into the sky. Without gravity, the Moon would float away too. And the planets would leave their orbits around the Sun.

The universe would become a much lonelier place.

I'm glad that gravity is keeping us on the Earth. Are you?

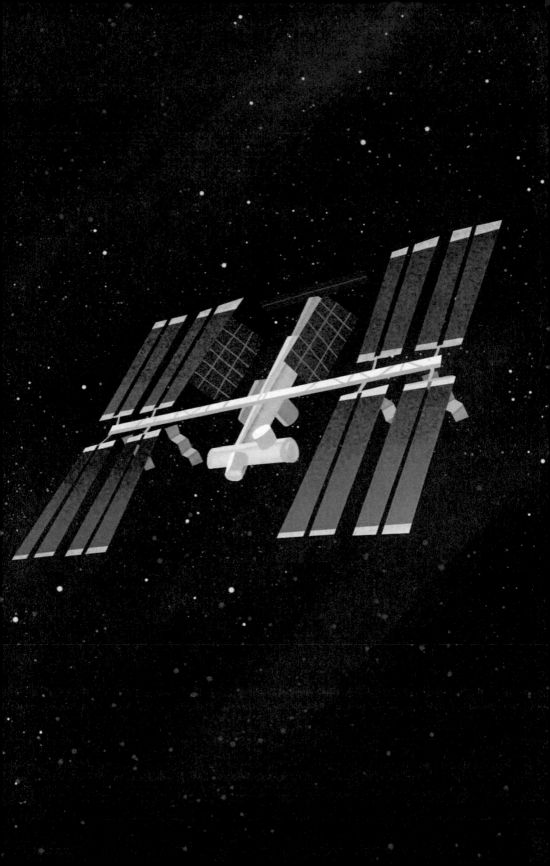

LIFE ON A SPACE STATION

The International Space Station is a laboratory that floats in space 400 kilometres above our heads. It is over 100 metres long and 73 metres wide—bigger than a football field. It orbits the Earth once every ninety minutes, travelling at a speed of 7.66 kilometres per second. The space station can hold up to six people at a time as they live and work there.

In 1998 the first section of the International Space Station was launched into orbit by astronauts on a space shuttle. The project was a worldwide collaboration between the European Space Agency, Japan, Canada, the United States and Russia. The station took a few years to build because every part had to be bolted together by astronauts wearing heavy spacesuits, working outside the safety of their spacecraft. These spacewalks were long and dangerous.

It's amazing to think that there are astronauts living up there right now! More than 200 people have done so, performing scientific experiments that test how plants, insects and the human body work in space. They also use equipment to study stars and galaxies, and the weather on Earth.

Astronauts can live on the International Space Station for between a few days and several months. The longest anyone has lived there continuously is more than a year. Living in Earth's orbit, however, is very different to living on Earth. Eating is quite tricky because all your food and drink floats. Showering is impossible because water drifts around in large droplets and will not fall onto your body. Instead, astronauts use damp cloths to wash themselves in space. Sleeping on a bed is also not possible, so astronauts float inside special sleeping bags.

And as for going to the toilet? Don't even ask! Let's just say that there are specially designed toilets that use suction instead of gravity to get rid of waste.

To measure the effects of space travel on human health, NASA, the US space agency, sent one of a pair of identical twins into space to measure the difference it made to his body. The other identical twin stayed at home and also took part in scientific testing. The results were very interesting.

Astronauts feel weightless in Earth's orbit, which can affect their bodies. The study found that the astronaut twin's muscles and bones became weaker because he was constantly floating weightless instead of using his muscles to support himself. The astronaut twin got taller too—because he was floating, his spine relaxed and the gaps between his bones, called vertebrae, got bigger. When the astronaut twin finally returned to Earth, he found it hard to stand up. It takes several months or even years for an astronaut's body to completely return to normal.

You can sometimes see the International Space Station passing high overhead. It looks like a really bright star that is moving steadily across the sky.

You can find out where the space station is at any time using an online tracker. Take a look when it next flies overhead—and don't forget to wave!

STOPPING COSMIC RAYS

lose your eyes. Take a deep breath. Now slowly let the breath out.

Did you know that in the time it took you to complete that one gentle cycle of breath, around 150 tiny subatomic particles, smaller than an atom, whizzed through your body close to the speed of light?

These amazing little particles are called cosmic rays. They can come from our Sun or they can come from somewhere deep in outer space, such as a supernova explosion, or a superheated region of spinning gas that is falling into a supermassive black hole in a distant galaxy. When one of these rays hits our atmosphere, it creates a shower of other particles which we give exotic names. These include pions (*pie-ons*), electrons, positrons and muons (*myoo-ons*). It's mind-boggling to think that, as we sit here on Earth, we are almost constantly drenched by matter and antimatter from space.

These cosmic ray showers might spritz us but they don't really hurt us. Very powerful cosmic rays can be harmful to our health, but luckily our atmosphere protects us from harm. The air acts as a filter, taking the most energetic cosmic rays and converting them into scatterings of less powerful particles. These then rain down onto the Earth, with many of them passing through our bodies like speedy little ghosts.

The atmosphere is not the only thing keeping us safe from a variety of powerful cosmic rays. We are also protected by an invisible force field—a magnetic shield that deflects many cosmic rays away from the Earth.

Above our atmosphere and the magnetic force field, cosmic rays pose more of a danger. In deep space, astronauts are especially vulnerable. The rays can cause damage to their DNA, not to mention disrupting electronic equipment such as cameras and computers.

Astronauts working in space have reported seeing green flashes at random times, which are thought to be caused by cosmic rays. The astronauts don't report seeing this green colour in the usual way, with light entering the pupil at the front of the eye. Instead, a flash of light is perceived when a cosmic ray flies harmlessly through the astronaut's head and interacts with the electrical circuits behind the eye. When these circuits are stimulated, a flash of green light is seen, whether or not the person's eyes are open—the flashes have even happened during sleep.

There is no easy way to get away from cosmic rays in space. We can shield a spacecraft by coating it with thick tubes of water or liquid hydrogen, but this makes the spacecraft very heavy and therefore expensive to launch. Another possibility is the creation of a magnetic shield that deflects the cosmic rays. But this solution has never been tested because it would use up a lot of electrical power and also be expensive.

A positive side to cosmic rays is that, here on Earth, they can be very helpful in working out the age of fossils and other animal remains.

When a cosmic ray hits a nitrogen atom in the atmosphere, it can transform the atom into a special type of radioactive carbon atom. Plants and animals absorb this special atom throughout their lives. Only when the plant or animal dies does this absorption stop. In the case of fossils, which might be millions of years old, scientists can measure the amount of these special carbon atoms that is still there. Since the atoms slowly decay at a specific rate, knowing how much of them is left allows scientists to figure out exactly how long ago the plant or animal died.

We call this technique carbon dating, and it is a great way of figuring out the history of life on Earth. That's how we know when the dinosaurs lived! Pretty cool, hey?

REAL ROCKET SCIENCE

Have you ever tried to push a really heavy shopping trolley in the supermarket? Have you noticed how the trolley pushes you backwards?

When you push on anything heavy—a house, a car, even the Earth—it automatically pushes back on you. This is not a decision that the object makes. It's just a natural reaction, which we call a force.

There are many forces. Friction is one. This force happens when two surfaces collide or rub against one another. Rubbing your hands together creates friction, as does sliding on a carpet on your knees (ouch!). As gas circles a black hole in space, friction generates heat.

Another force you might be familiar with is magnetism. Many objects in space are magnetic, including the Earth and the stars. Magnetism in the Sun generates lots of exciting activity. These include solar flares, when the Sun expels hot gas, and sunspots, which are cooler patches on the Sun's surface caused by magnetic fields.

Gravity is a pulling force. The Earth is so big that there is a very strong gravitational pull between it and your body. That's why you stay on the ground instead of floating around in the air. This is also why you can't jump over a house or leap into outer space. It takes a big force to jump into space. A REALLY big force.

We can create an enormous force like this if we use a rocket.

In a rocket, we light fuel and create a chemical reaction. Whether the fuel is solid or liquid, this chemical reaction quickly turns it into an extremely hot gas. This causes the gas to expand and it shoots very quickly out of an enormous nozzle at the back of the rocket.

It's like a shopping trolley (well, sort of)—if you push something, it will push you back. The automatic reaction to the gas pushing its way out of the rocket is a push in the other direction. As the gas moves backwards, the rocket flies forward. That is how rockets work.

You might wonder why you can't just fly an aeroplane into space. Wouldn't that be simpler and cheaper? It sure would! But an aeroplane needs to be immersed in air for it to successfully fly.

As a plane moves forward, air moves around its wings. The shape of the wing is specially designed to make air move faster on the top of the wing and slower on the bottom. This difference in air speed above and below the wings creates an upwards push. This is what keeps aeroplanes in the sky.

Aeroplanes work brilliantly in our atmosphere, but in space there is no air. That's why we use rockets in space.

In the future, we may not even need to use rockets. One new idea on powering spaceships involves using lasers on the ground to push them along like sailing boats on a breezy day.

If we can work out how to invent new spacecraft, we might travel to other planets faster than we think. For now though, we rely on rockets to get humans, their food and their scientific equipment into space.

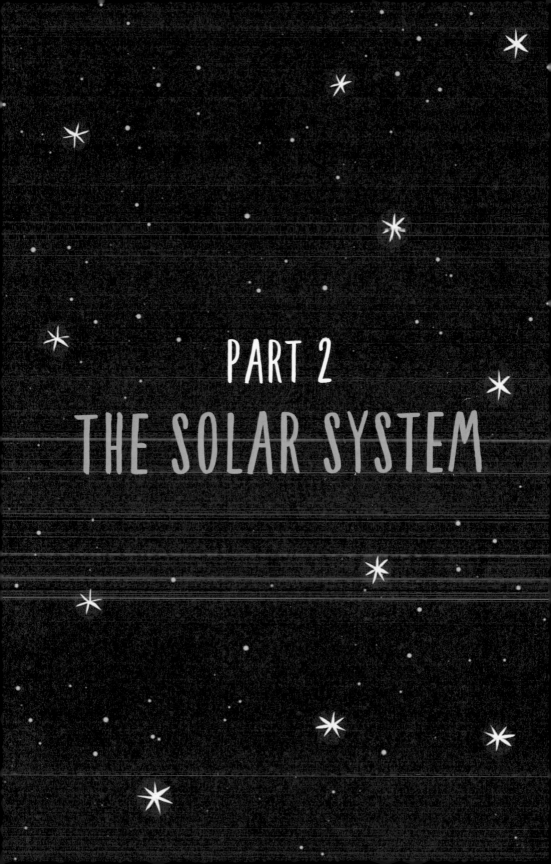

PART 2
THE SOLAR SYSTEM

OUR VERY OWN STAR

The Sun is a bright, yellow globule of gas shining brilliantly in space. It warms and nourishes our planet, helping plants and animals to grow. However, the Sun can also burn our skin if we're not careful to cover up and stay in the shade. Of course, that's nothing to how hot it would feel if you could get much closer to it.

The hottest part of the Sun is right in the middle of it. This is called the core, and it's where tiny particles, like the protons and neutrons that make up atoms, crash together and generate vast amounts of heat and light. The core of the Sun is its engine, burning at an incredible temperature of 15 million degrees Celsius.

Just outside the core of the Sun is a layer of gas called the radiative zone. This layer is a little cooler than the core—it's only 7 million degrees Celsius there. This gas is so busy and chaotic that heat and light take millions of years to shove their way out of this zone.

A little further out is the Sun's convection zone. This is where hot gas bubbles towards the exterior of the star before slowly cooling and sinking down once again. The temperature of this region varies from 2 million degrees Celsius at the bottom to a few thousand degrees Celsius at the top.

Above this simmering region of gas is the so-called 'surface' of the Sun, the photosphere. The Sun doesn't have a solid surface like the Earth. It only has a gas layer that we can see when we look at the Sun with special cameras, which astronomers use to safely take and view pictures. This is very important—never look at the Sun directly or through a telescope as this can badly damage your eyesight.

The temperature at the Sun's surface is around 5800 degrees Celsius, although it also has cooler patches called sunspots, which are only 3800 degrees Celsius. Sunspots look dark against the Sun's fiery yellow exterior. They are cooler than their surroundings because they are places where strong magnetic fields make it hard for the hot gas to rise to the surface.

The Sun also has an atmosphere, but it is not a pleasant, breathable atmosphere like ours. There are no clouds, or birds or aeroplanes flying around. The sky is not blue, like on the Earth. The Sun's atmosphere is extremely hot and filled with tiny particles whizzing about at incredible speeds. The lower part of this atmosphere has a temperature of around 5000 degrees Celsius, but the upper region is heated to more than 2 million degrees Celsius.

We don't know why the Sun's atmosphere is so hot, even though we have sent spacecraft to study it at close range. Sometimes it gets even hotter, such as when the Sun creates a solar flare. This is when the Sun burps and a big cloud of flaming gas flies all the way to the Earth, firing tiny particles into our upper atmosphere. This generates amazing curtains of shimmering green and red light in our night sky, which are called an aurora.

The aurora near the North Pole is often called the northern lights. You can see this in Greenland, Canada and parts of Russia and Scandinavia. The aurora near the South Pole is called the southern lights. This is mostly visible in Antarctica but is also seen in South America, New Zealand and in Australia—in parts of southern Victoria and Tasmania.

Considering how hot and dangerous it is, we are very lucky to live around such a well-behaved star as the Sun. What would we do without it?

MERCURY—THE PLANET THAT HUGS THE SUN

Orbiting very close to the Sun is what has to be the bravest planet in our solar system, Mercury, which is heated ferociously by its neighbour. But Mercury is actually only the second-hottest planet. The honour of hottest planet goes to Venus, which has a thick atmosphere of carbon dioxide that keeps it unbearably warm year-round.

The temperature on Mercury, the smallest planet in our solar system (it's only one-third the diameter of Earth), is extremely variable. It ranges from 450 degrees Celsius during the day to minus 180 degrees Celsius at night. These extremes occur because Mercury experiences very long, hot days facing the Sun and long cold nights spent in darkness. Because the planet's orbit around the Sun takes eighty-eight days and it spins on its axis quite slowly, there are only one-and-a-half days every year on Mercury—that means lots of birthdays! A layer of air around a planet traps heat like a blanket and equalises the temperature across its surface, but this doesn't happen on Mercury because it has almost no atmosphere.

Mercury is a rocky planet, just like the Earth, Venus and Mars. Its surface is pockmarked with craters, just like our Moon. These have happened over thousands of millions of years as the rocks flying around our solar system smack into the surface of Mercury. A lack of wind and running water means that these scars have not eroded but rather will stay there forever.

Mercury is also marked by some enormous asteroid impacts that happened around 4 billion years ago, when the planet was very young. Asteroids are bigger than meteorites, so they cause even bigger craters. But despite having had big collisions in its early life, which can sometimes throw off material that forms moons, Mercury wanders alone.

Mercury doesn't have a circular orbit. It moves around the Sun on a slightly egg-shaped path. When it is closest to our star, Mercury zips by it at a distance of only 47 million kilometres. When it is the furthest away from the Sun and moving more slowly, the distance is 70 million kilometres.

This variation in orbital speed leads to some strange behaviour on the surface of Mercury. Because the planet is orbiting the Sun so fast, at times the Sun will rise on Mercury and then set again, before rising fully and the day beginning. Weird or what?!

You can sometimes see Mercury in the morning or evening sky, but only for a short time just after sunset or just before sunrise. It looks like a little star in the night sky, always hugging the Sun. I've seen it once or twice and it was very exciting.

The best way to find Mercury is to look in the 'sky guide' section of an online astronomy magazine, or use a night sky app, which will tell you how and when to see this planet. Good luck!

VENUS—CLOUDY WITH A CHANCE OF ACID

O ut there in the solar system is a rocky planet that is almost
exactly the same size as the Earth. Our planet's twin, which is
called Venus, orbits the Sun every 225 days—that equals one
year on Venus. But Venus is by no means the Earth's *identical*
twin. The differences between our planets are quite dramatic.

For starters, Venus is exceedingly hot. I mean unimaginably,
hotter-than-an-oven, blistering, flamingly so. The average temperature on the planet's surface is 462 degrees Celsius, which is
easily hot enough to melt metal. And this incredible heat isn't
generated just because Venus is closer than we are to the Sun,
although that does help.

The main reason for the planet's high temperature is that it
has a very unusual atmosphere, one that is more than 96 per cent
carbon dioxide. On Earth, carbon dioxide only makes up 0.02 per

cent of our atmosphere, yet this still creates a 'greenhouse effect'—the carbon dioxide in the atmosphere traps the Sun's heat and warms the Earth. The same thing happens on Venus, but on a much more massive scale.

The atmosphere of Venus is also incredibly dense. It has a crushing pressure ninety times that of Earth's. This is an overwhelmingly dangerous environment in which humans could not survive for long, even in specially modified spacesuits.

Within the atmosphere of Venus are thick clouds. These are not made of water droplets like those here on Earth. They are made of highly dangerous sulphuric acid, which would burn our skin on contact! Nope, Venus is really not a good place to visit.

Venus' clouds are so thick that we can't see through them. So the only way to study the surface of the planet is to use spacecraft that bounce radar signals off it and measure how long they take to return. Detailed radar mapping from orbiting spacecraft has revealed more than 1000 volcanoes.

Another big difference is that the Earth spins on its axis once every twenty-four hours—that's one day on Earth. But Venus does so very slowly, spinning on its axis only once every 243 Earth days. Just to make that weirder, a day on Venus (243 Earth days for the planet to rotate once on its axis) is longer than a year on Venus (225 Earth days for the planet to orbit the Sun).

Venus also spins backwards compared with most of the other planets in the solar system. We don't really know why, but one theory is that it collided with another planet a very long time ago, flipping it upside down!

You may not ever visit this planet of acid rain, crushing pressure and searing heat, but you can see it from the safety of home. Venus is often called the 'morning star' or the 'evening star' because it shines brightly before sunrise or after sunset, usually well into twilight. It is not really a star, of course, but it does look like one, so the names have stuck. Venus seems so bright—much brighter than any star—because of the sunlight that's reflected by its thick clouds.

Have you ever seen Venus, shining brighter than the stars? If you haven't, or if you want to see it again, you can download an app to help you find it in the night sky, along with other stars and planets.

THE EARTH AND THE SUN —
THE BEST OF FRIENDS

A very long time ago, in a place called the solar system, the Earth and the Sun were born. All the other planets in our solar system were born there too. You could say they were like sisters and brothers.

The Sun and all the planets were made in the same place, from a single cloud of gas and dust that was floating in space. We call this cloud a nebula. Space is full of these clouds. They float between the stars and fill parts of our galaxy with beautiful colours. You can see a few nebulae with a small telescope. One of these is the Orion Nebula, which is an amazing cloud of dust, part of which has the shape of a horse's head.

The nebula that made our Sun and planets was, at the time, very old. Around 5 billion years ago, it began pulling together by the force of gravity. It began spinning too. In the centre of this spinning cloud, an enormous ball of gas started to take shape—a giant globule of hydrogen that gained more and more bulk. Meanwhile, the nebula kept spinning and getting smaller and smaller as gravity gripped it tighter and tighter.

As particles in the nebula rubbed together, it became very hot in the middle. When its core temperature became hot enough to burn, it began to shine brightly. This was our Sun, a yellow star.

The Sun doesn't burn like a fire, which uses fuel and oxygen to generate heat. Rather, it generates heat by building bigger chemicals from smaller ones. As hydrogen atoms join together to make helium atoms in the core of our Sun, huge amounts of energy, heat and light are released.

At the same time as the Sun was forming, the planets began to take shape. Gravity grabbed handfuls of gas and dust from the spinning cloud and started rolling them into little balls that got bigger and bigger as they spun around and collected more gas and dust. The ones that formed further away from the Sun became gas giants—Jupiter, Saturn, Uranus and Neptune. The rocky planets—Mercury, Venus, Earth and Mars—were shaped closer to the Sun. Since the cloud was spinning, all the planets began orbiting the Sun as they formed—as they continue to do today.

Our star shone its immense heat and light onto the planets. Some planets, like Mercury and Venus, were too hot to host living things. Others, like Saturn and Neptune, were too cold. One planet—Earth—was just the right temperature for the creation of life. From our primitive planet's bacteria, bugs, plants, fish and animals developed, and the Earth eventually had an abundance of living creatures. And every day, the shining Sun gave us the warmth and light that we needed to live.

In return, the Earth has remained very loyal to the Sun. It holds to it tightly with the force of gravity, circling once around the Sun each and every year, never wandering too far away.

The Sun and the Earth really are the best of friends.

SEEING RED ON MARS

Mars, the fourth planet from the Sun, is called the red planet. Its colour originates from iron oxide (or rust) in its soil. This is the same chemical that produces the red colour in the soil of many outback regions of Australia.

So far we've only sent robotic spacecraft to Mars, although there are now plans to design a new spacecraft that is capable of taking astronauts there. If this is successful, it is possible that we might send people to Mars within the next few years. Have you ever wondered what it would be like to go on a trip to Mars?

For starters, how long would it take to get there? Well, this would depend on where the Earth and Mars were in their orbits. Sometimes the two planets are quite close to one another, and at other times they are at opposite points in their orbits around the Sun. On average, the Earth and Mars are 228 million kilometres apart. Based on the average speed of a spacecraft, it would take around seven months to reach the red planet from here.

Once you got there, communication with Earth would be difficult. Imagine that you've found an engine leak and you need to talk to mission control to try and solve the problem. Mars is so far away from Earth that it would take on average twelve-and-a-half minutes for your voice signal to travel home. Once mission control had replied to the message, it would take another twelve-and-a-half minutes for their response to reach you. That's a pretty long wait for such a vital piece of information.

Your body would feel pretty different on Mars too. Mars is half the diameter of the Earth, and two-and-a-half times smaller by volume. Its small size means that everything would feel two-and-a-half times lighter there. On its surface, you'd bounce around instead of walking, and objects would feel easier to lift and carry.

Mars would not be an easy place to inhabit. Its weather is pretty wild. The temperature there averages minus 63 degrees Celsius, but it can vary from minus 140 degrees Celsius to 30 degrees Celsius. Also, the atmosphere of Mars is 100 times thinner than the Earth's and mostly made up of carbon dioxide. Not only is it impossible to breathe, it is also too thin to effectively shield you from radiation (called cosmic rays) from space. You would need to spend all your time in a pressurised spacesuit.

The sky on Mars would look very different. During the day, the sky would be orangey-red due to all the dust blowing around the atmosphere. At night, or when the dust was not too thick, you would see Mars' two moons, Phobos (*foe-boss*) and

Deimos (*dee-moss*). Can you imagine having two moons in the sky above you?

The larger moon, Phobos, is 22 kilometres across and circles Mars very quickly, making one orbit every seven hours and thirty-nine minutes. Twice every day, Phobos rises in the east, travels across the sky for around four hours, and sets in the west.

On most days there would be a transit of Phobos, which is a bit like a solar eclipse. On Mars, this transit would be a little different though. Phobos would pass directly in front of the Sun and block out most of its light. The sky would darken for about thirty seconds, then Phobos would move on and full sunlight would return.

The smaller moon, Deimos, is much further away than Phobos from the surface of Mars. It is also much smaller than Phobos—it's 12.6 kilometres across—meaning that it would appear very small in Mars' sky. Instead of a moon, you would see what resembled a very bright star. Deimos takes just over one day to orbit the planet, and when it passed in front of the Sun, it would be too small to really notice.

The moons of Mars would make for some fascinating stargazing, but the conditions on the planet would make it a difficult place to live. If you were designing a house for living on Mars, what special features would it need to have?

HOW JUPITER GOT
ITS STRIPES

Jupiter is the biggest planet in our solar system—in fact, it is 1300 times bigger than the Earth. We have learned a lot about Jupiter in the past forty years by sending spacecraft from Earth. These spacecraft have used robotic cameras and conducted scientific experiments on board to study Jupiter's atmosphere and find out more about this enormous gas giant.

Astronauts have never been to Jupiter because it would take several years to travel there, and once you got there it would be very difficult to slow down your spacecraft, turn around and travel back to Earth. But if you could travel to Jupiter, what would it be like?

Unlike the Earth, which is mostly made of, well, earth, Jupiter is mainly made of gas. And of course, gas is soft and squidgy and you can't stand on it at all. Deep below the gas clouds is a ball of liquid that is spinning around quite fast. Even further down is the core of the planet. We're not certain exactly what's down there because we have never seen the inside of Jupiter, but we get clues from the experiments done on the visiting spacecraft. These suggest that it may hide a ball of solid rock bigger than the Earth.

Whether it is rocky or not, the core of Jupiter is VERY hot. Experiments show that the temperature in Jupiter's middle is around 30 000 degrees Celsius. That is far hotter than fire, so the core wouldn't be a great place to visit. Another reason to stay away is the immense weight of the planet's atmosphere. The pressure is so significant that you and your spacecraft would be completely squashed.

But Jupiter is beautiful from afar. The planet's thick clouds give it a stripy appearance, like a tiger. Scientists are still working to find out exactly how Jupiter got its stripes. One idea is that gravity from the planet's many moons is pulling on the gas, making it line up in stripes. Another possible explanation is that bands of gas in the atmosphere are either rising (warm air) or falling (cool air), which gives them different colours.

Jupiter's atmosphere isn't just stripy—it's spotty too! The largest is a massive storm called the Great Red Spot, which is three times the size of the Earth. It swirls around in a circle, with winds that could knock a house down, travelling at more than 400 kilometres per hour. Scientists are still trying to understand why this spot is red. We think the reddish gas is created when sunlight shines on chemicals high up in the atmosphere of Jupiter.

Zooming out from Jupiter's spotty and stripy atmosphere, we come to its enormous family of moons. The planet has an incredible seventy-nine moons, with new ones being discovered all the time. Jupiter also has a system of very faint rings, each made up of millions of tiny pieces of dust that are orbiting the planet. The rings were discovered forty years ago by *Voyager 1*, which was the first spacecraft to take close-up pictures of Jupiter.

If you flew to Jupiter on a spacecraft, what would you like to discover?

SATURN HAS A NICE RING TO IT

There is a planet in our solar system that wears the most glamorous jewellery you could imagine—glittering golden rings. Which one am I talking about? It's Saturn of course.

Most of Saturn is made up of the lightest gases in the universe, hydrogen and helium, which meander above a layer of liquid hydrogen and a small solid core. This makes the planet so buoyant that it would float on water—if you could find a swimming pool big enough to hold it!

The atmosphere of Saturn is a fascinating place. At a chilly minus 185 degrees Celsius, it is very cold. There are bands of swirling clouds in the upper atmosphere that create stripes of various colours. These are not normal clouds of water like we have on Earth, though. They are made up of many different chemicals.

The wind speeds in the upper atmosphere of Saturn are as high as 1800 kilometres per hour, which is twice the speed of an aeroplane. Every thirty years or so, at the peak of Saturn's summer, a great white spot forms in the clouds. Similar to Jupiter's Great Red Spot, the Great White Spot is a storm thousands of kilometres wide that rages for several months. Its clouds extend into the lower atmosphere, where wind speeds reach up to 500 kilometres per hour.

When we sent a spacecraft to fly past Saturn in 1980, we managed to photograph an enormous hexagon shape in the clouds around the planet's north pole. It is wider than the Earth and 300 kilometres high, and its colour changes from blue to orange depending on the season. The amazing shape of this cloud feature is thought to be caused by the gases in the atmosphere circling the planet at different speeds.

But Saturn is most famous for its spectacular system of rings. These rings are immediately obvious when you look at the planet through a telescope. Breathtakingly beautiful, they are made of water ice (rather than ices made of different chemicals) along with solid particles, ranging from grains of dust to pebbles, and rocks as big as cars.

Like Saturn itself, the rings shine not by their own light but by reflected light from the Sun. They are very big, around 120 000 kilometres wide, but they are super-thin—around 20 metres wide. We don't know for sure how they got there, but it is possible that they are the remnants of a moon that was destroyed by a collision long ago.

Speaking of which, Saturn has sixty-two moons. Around half of these are relatively small, less than 200 kilometres across, and have irregular shapes—lumpy like a potato. Many orbit Saturn at strange angles; some even orbit backwards compared with the others. The irregular-shaped moons may be asteroids, big rocks left over from the formation of the solar system that have been captured by Saturn's gravity. The larger, spherical moons are rocky and cratered, with some covered in oceans and ice made up of water and other chemicals.

The largest of all Saturn's moons is Titan (*tie-tun*). Even bigger than Mercury, Titan is a wondrous place. It has a thick atmosphere, a rocky surface and oceans of liquid methane. There are many complex chemicals in its atmosphere that are thought to be the building blocks of life. The trouble is, it is very cold, which makes it difficult for large biological chemicals to form and survive. So we haven't found evidence of life just yet.

Enceladus (*en-cellar-dus*) is another large moon that could possibly host life. It is covered in ice, with deep oceans underneath. In places, this hidden water is heated and shoots up high into the atmosphere. Interestingly, the water contains organic chemicals that may hint at the presence of life.

Teams of scientists have proposed sending a spacecraft to Enceladus in the next few years to hunt for life. If you were in charge of this mission, where would you begin your search?

URANUS IS FULL OF GAS

Uranus is the seventh planet from the Sun, coming after Jupiter and Saturn. It is a gas planet, and a big one at that—sixty-three Earths could fit inside. Uranus is also very far away from us, between 2.5 and 3 billion kilometres. The distance to the planet changes because the Earth and Uranus are both orbiting the Sun. When the two planets are on the same side of the Sun, they are closer together, and when they are on opposite sides of the Sun, they are further apart.

About once a year, Uranus is fully illuminated by the Sun. At this time, the planet can be seen faintly with just your eyes, without using a telescope. We call this the 'opposition' of Uranus because it is opposite the Sun in the sky. Sometimes, when Uranus is far from the Earth, it appears smaller and fainter. At other times, when it's close to the Sun, it appears bigger and brighter. The next time it will appear at its brightest will be in the year 2050. How old will you be in 2050?

The first people to notice Uranus assumed it was just another star. But once astronomers took a closer look with their telescopes, they saw that Uranus seemed bigger and fuzzier than a star, which led them to believe it could be a comet. To check whether this was true, astronomers followed Uranus' motion through the sky and calculated its orbit around the Sun. They were quite surprised to find that the orbit was not egg-shaped, like that of a comet, but almost circular, like that of a planet. It had taken a while, but scientists had finally realised that Uranus was a planet.

We now know that Uranus is a gas giant planet made up of hydrogen, helium and a little bit of methane. Its pale blue colour is caused by light scattering off the methane ice crystals high up in its atmosphere. Only one spacecraft has ever visited Uranus up close. This was the NASA space probe *Voyager 2*, which took photographs and measured the planet's atmosphere and clouds in 1986.

Unlike Jupiter and Saturn, the atmosphere of Uranus is quite plain. For most of the year, we don't see the stripy coloured clouds and the giant storms of the other gas giants. That's because the inside of Uranus is quite cold, leading to a lack of cloud patterns at lower altitudes. In fact, the planet's interior is made up of an icy liquid, like a slushy. Experiments on Earth that have replicated the conditions on Uranus suggest that there might even be diamond icebergs floating on the surface of the liquid. Imagine that!

Despite the plainness of Uranus' atmosphere, its high-up regions can produce phenomenal wind speeds. The jet streams there blow as fast as 900 kilometres per hour, which is more than twice the maximum hurricane winds ever recorded on Earth. These jet streams are thought to be driven by water vapour that is heated by sunlight and transports the heat to the upper atmosphere.

Outside the atmosphere of the planet is a set of faint rings, made up of tiny, dark particles of dust. They may have been created when two Uranian moons collided long ago. There are plenty of moons left, though—at least twenty-seven of them. The largest ones are called Miranda, Ariel, Umbriel, Titania and Oberon, which are made of rock and ice.

The strangest thing about Uranus is that it spins on its side. Unlike the other planets, whose poles face up and down, Uranus' north and south poles point in the same direction as its orbit. We think this may have been caused by an Earth-sized planet crashing into Uranus early on, when the solar system was being formed.

Remember how the tilt of Earth's axis causes our seasons? Well, Uranus has some very strange seasons due to the planet having been flipped onto its side.

Imagine that you are at the south pole of Uranus. As the planet does one orbit of the Sun, which takes eighty-four years, you'll experience forty-two years of continuous sunshine followed by forty-two years of complete darkness. Even away from the poles the weather is strange. In summer, most of the planet is either completely dark or completely light. This lasts for about twenty-one years, until the planet has moved far enough in its orbit for its axis to be edge-on to the Sun.

All in all, Uranus is pretty weird.

NEPTUNE—THE UNSEEN PLANET

The eighth and final planet in our solar system is Neptune. It is the hide-and-seek champion of our family of planets, a master of concealment and stealth, unidentified by humans until the mid-nineteenth century. Of course, it is also so far away from the Earth that it can't be seen without a telescope. That's the main reason it managed to creep around our solar system, virtually unnoticed, for so long.

Still, in science, it pays to pay attention. One day, a small group of smart astronomers who were making careful records of the orbits of the planets noticed that the blue gas giant Uranus was being pulled off course. They wondered what could be causing Uranus to deviate from its predictable path around the Sun. The most likely thing, the astronomers decided, was an unseen planet orbiting beyond Uranus.

These astronomers got to work to find the culprit. But instead of searching the night sky using their telescopes—the sky is very big, after all—they used maths to figure out how big this unseen planet must be and where it might sit in the sky. Those calculations were a great success because within weeks, the planet in question had been identified as a tiny blue point of light. Neptune had been found!

Neptune is a gas giant, just like Uranus. It is heavier than Uranus but physically smaller, meaning it is made of slightly different stuff. Neptune has a hot liquid ocean full of water, ammonia and methane. Underneath this is a heavy core that is probably made of iron and nickel, just like the core of the Earth.

Neptune has an amazing dark-blue colour. This is caused by methane and other gases in its upper atmosphere that absorb red light and reflect blue light. This blue atmosphere is the coldest place on any planet, at a bone-freezing minus 220 degrees Celsius.

Neptune's atmosphere is very dynamic. We see fierce storms there, similar to the cyclones on Earth and Jupiter. Against the background of Neptune's blue atmosphere, these storms look like black spots. They seem dark because the storms happen in the lower regions of the atmosphere. This disrupts the upper atmosphere, which is usually the bright bit that we see. And so the spots look darker than the surrounding regions.

The biggest storm we have ever seen on Neptune was GDS-89, or the Great Dark Spot. This gigantic storm was studied up-close by the *Voyager 2* spacecraft that flew past Neptune in 1989. This revealed that GDS-89 was the same size as the Earth.

The Great Dark Spot also had extremely strong winds of up to 2200 kilometres per hour, the fastest recorded in the solar system. By 1994, when astronomers again looked at Neptune with the Hubble Space Telescope, the Great Dark Spot had vanished.

Neptune is not alone out there. It has a family of fourteen moons. Most of them are small and lumpy, but there is a big, spherical moon called Triton, which orbits backwards around Neptune. This suggests it may have started off as a dwarf planet— like Pluto—but was captured at some point in the past by Neptune's gravitational pull.

Triton is a little larger than Pluto, with a diameter of just over 2000 kilometres. It is a volcanic world that is covered in ice and has a thin atmosphere. It has vents called geysers that regularly erupt, spewing out clouds of gas and dust that stretch up to 8 kilometres high! This has contributed to Triton's thin atmosphere, which is composed of nitrogen, with tiny amounts of carbon dioxide and methane.

Neptune and its moons are fascinating places. But due to their great distance from Earth, they haven't been studied at close range since *Voyager 2* visited thirty years ago. Let's hope that in the years to come, we will visit once again to learn more about the outermost planet in our solar system.

THE DARK WORLD OF PLUTO

When I was a child, there were nine planets in our solar system. The furthest from the Sun was Pluto. A tiny, far-flung and rocky world, Pluto was discovered in 1930 when astronomers noticed a teensy dot of light moving slowly across the sky.

We now know that Pluto is part of a large swarm of minor rocky bodies beyond the orbit of Neptune, called the Kuiper Belt. That's why Pluto is not regarded as a full-blown planet anymore. Rather, it is now officially known as a dwarf planet.

Pluto's surface is a frozen mixture of ice basins and cratered rocky regions. There are also some floating mountains made of water ice. And there are giant features that look like volcanoes, except that these enormous fissures erupt with flows of ice instead of lava.

Pluto also has five known moons. The largest is called Charon, which is almost a twin of Pluto. The smaller moons are called Styx, Nix, Hydra and Kerberos.

Pluto is so far away that if you were visiting it during the daytime, the Sun would only look as bright as a full moon. It is a dark world. A dark and fascinating world.

ASTEROID BELTS AND ICY CLOUDS

Our solar system is best known for the blazing heat of the Sun and the eight remarkable planets that orbit around it, but they are not the whole story. Most of the objects in the solar system are smaller rocky and icy bodies that float between the planets.

Many of these bodies lie in the giant swarm of rocks circling the Sun between the orbits of Mars and Jupiter—the asteroid belt. Most of the rocks here are a few metres in size, but the largest one, called Ceres, is a whopper at 946 kilometres across. Other asteroids travel around the Sun in clumps, shepherded by Jupiter's gravity.

Throughout the history of the solar system, many asteroids have collided with the planets and created enormous craters—including on Earth. It is thought that a giant asteroid impact

66 million years ago led to a dramatic change in the Earth's climate that in turn wiped out the dinosaurs. Remnants of the 150-kilometre-wide crater left by this event can still be seen near the coast of Mexico.

Smaller asteroids the size of a car vaporise harmlessly in our atmosphere at least once a year. And around 100 tonnes of rock dust, called meteors, burn up in our atmosphere every day. That's the equivalent of sixty-seven cars in weight!

Another source of loose rocks in our solar system is the Kuiper Belt, which lies outside the orbit of Neptune. This is a large swarm of around 100 000 minor planets stretching towards the edge of the solar system. We can't know for sure, but it is likely that these minor planets, many of which are more than 100 kilometres across, are rocks left over from the formation of the solar system.

Zooming out much further, far beyond the Kuiper Belt, we find a spherical bank of icy and rocky bodies called the Oort Cloud. The Oort Cloud is far from the Sun, so the rocks are covered in thick ice made up of water, carbon dioxide, carbon monoxide, ammonia and methane.

Sometimes, one of these icy rocks becomes dislodged from the Oort Cloud by a nearby gravitational disturbance, perhaps when a planet comes near. We call this a comet. As a comet begins its long journey towards the inner solar system, it eventually gets close to the Sun, where it is heated by sunlight and begins to melt. The ice on its surface forms a cloud of gases that stream away from the Sun—what we call the comet's tail.

A typical comet from the Oort Cloud may take thousands of years to orbit the Sun. It will spend the vast majority of its time in the freezing cold of space, far from any source of heat or light. Only for a few short weeks will it visit the Sun and shine brightly. After that, it will swing back around the Sun and disappear into the darkness.

In 1994, a comet called Shoemaker-Levy 9 hit Jupiter. It had been travelling towards the Sun when it was deflected by Jupiter's gravity, and it then found itself orbiting the planet for several years. But the orbit was unstable and the comet moved slowly towards the planet, breaking up into many smaller fragments. Eventually it dived straight into Jupiter's clouds and finally crashed into the planet.

This event was amazing because astronomers managed to take photographs of it as it happened. The comet left dark impact scars on Jupiter's cloud belts that lasted for several months. A few years later, a similar collision between a large asteroid and Jupiter was seen. It left a hole in the clouds the size of the Pacific Ocean.

It's lucky that Jupiter has such a strong gravitational pull. Many scientists think that this keeps the Earth safe from larger asteroids that may otherwise collide with our own planet. Three cheers for Jupiter!

HOW MUCH WOULD YOU WEIGH ON OTHER PLANETS?

Here on planet Earth, your feet are planted firmly on the ground. Yet with a bit of effort you can easily run, and jump, and bounce on a trampoline. But what would it be like on other planets? Elsewhere in the solar system, how much would you weigh, and how high could you jump?

Imagine for a moment that you weigh 30 kilograms on Earth. Now pretend that you've figured out a way to heat-proof yourself and it's possible for you to visit the Sun. If you were able to visit the Sun and stand on a scale there, it would read a whopping 812 kilograms. That's right—you would weigh almost as much as a small car weighs on Earth! Because the Sun is so much heavier than the Earth, its gravitational pull on your body is far stronger.

On Mercury, the smallest planet in the solar system, you would weigh a mere 11.3 kilograms. Carrying only one-third of the weight you have on Earth, you'd be able to bounce pretty high there—about twice as high as you could manage here.

Moving on to Venus, you would feel quite normal there, weighing in at 27.2 kilograms. On Mars, however, your weight would drop to 11.3 kilograms, the same as on Mercury. Although Mars is quite a bit bigger than Mercury, it is made of lighter stuff, so its gravity is pretty much the same.

What about the gas giant planets?

As you travel through the solar system, Jupiter would come up first. Here you would feel really sluggish, dragging your heels at a hefty 75.8 kilograms. It would feel like you were giving a teenager a piggyback. Not much jumping to be done!

Next up would be Saturn. On this gas giant, you'd only weigh 31.9 kilograms because Saturn is made of very light gas. You'd feel pretty normal on the ringed planet, but you'd fall through the ground pretty quickly. Splosh!

On Uranus and Neptune, your weight would not be that dissimilar to how much you weigh on Earth—26.6 kilograms and 33.7 kilograms respectively. Your jumping would feel pretty normal (although again, on these gas planets there would be no place to land).

Finally, what if you visited the dwarf planet Pluto?

Pluto is a very small body, six times smaller than the Earth, and even smaller than our Moon. Its compact size means that you would only weigh 4 kilograms there. That's right—FOUR kilograms.

On Pluto, you could jump around 7 metres high! Imagine the view from up there. Your jump would be spectacular. It would take you around nine seconds to slowly float through the air. Just think of the acrobatics you could get up to.

Which planet would you most like to visit?

THE SECRET LIFE OF THE SUN

Nearly five billion years ago, the Sun was born in a nursery for stars. It formed gradually from a giant cloud of gas and dust—a nebula—that was floating in space. Gravity carefully pulled together clumps of the gas into tight balls, like dough being gathered by the skilled hands of a baker. These balls grew hotter and hotter, and eventually each one became a star.

So the Sun was just one of many stars born in this cloud. Its brothers and sisters, the other stars formed at the same time, have since moved on to live in different parts of the Milky Way.

In the core of our star are tiny specks of hydrogen gas—its fuel. These crash head-on, sticking together and then building bigger particles, the cores of helium atoms. This process, called nuclear fusion, releases vast quantities of heat and light. This is what makes the Sun shine.

The Sun is a yellow dwarf star. That means it is not too big and not too small, just average-sized. That's lucky for us, because very big stars have unpredictable lives.

The Sun burns about 500 million metric tons of hydrogen every second, which enables its light to fall steadily onto the Earth and feed the abundance of life that grows on our planet. A star like ours is big enough that it can burn like this for around 10 billion years. But our Sun is currently around halfway through its life. In another five billion years or so, it will start to run out of fuel.

Eventually, the Sun's core will have no hydrogen left to burn. This will leave it powerless, like a car that has run out of petrol. The Sun will temporarily stop shining and the core will shrink, pulled together by gravity, and then the helium will start to burn. Since helium burns more ferociously than hydrogen, the outer layers of gas will expand and the Sun will become a red giant star.

This red giant will be absolutely enormous! It will expand to 250 times its current size, its outer layers engulfing the Earth.

Once all the helium has burned up, the Sun's core will collapse again. It will squash down into a tiny white dwarf star the size of the Earth—a white dwarf does not burn gas but simply glows faintly with its residual heat, for billions of years. Meanwhile, the outer layers of the Sun will slowly expand and blow off into space, shining faintly as a beautiful nebula in the night sky.

This is the Sun's life. It begins as a cloud of gas and it ends as a cloud of gas. From a yellow dwarf, it becomes a red giant, and finally a tiny, faint white dwarf. The Sun then gently shines on for what seems like an eternity, with memories of a life well spent giving warmth to the creatures of the Earth.

PART 3
EXTRASOLAR SPACE

PULSARS—THE INCREDIBLE SPINNING STARS

I n 1967, a university student named Jocelyn Bell was studying the night sky through a really big telescope in Cambridge, England, when she came across a very curious object. She noticed that although it wasn't very bright, it was flashing on and off at an astonishing rate.

At first, Jocelyn and her fellow scientists had no idea why this object in the sky was flashing, or what it was—no-one had ever seen anything like it before. They gave it the nickname LGM-1, which stood for 'little green men'. They joked that the flashing light could be a signal from other intelligent beings out in space. Jokes aside, they thought that maybe there were other life forms out there in the Milky Way that were trying to send them a message, or make contact.

After further study, though, the scientists found that the signal was not coming from aliens at all. It was actually coming from a tiny star that was spinning incredibly fast, almost two times every second. What's more, this star wasn't glowing in all directions like a normal star. Instead, it was shining two powerful beams of light and radio waves from its north and south poles. The scientists worked out that each time the star spun around, a beam would cross the Earth's path and a brilliant flash could be seen.

The star was emitting pulses of energy, like a heartbeat, so it was called a pulsar.

Since then, we've discovered that some pulsars spin even faster than two rotations every second. The fastest we've seen so far spins at 700 000 kilometres per second. That's 24 per cent of the speed of light!

Pulsars have to be some of the WEIRDEST stars in the whole universe.

Instead of being made of gas like normal stars, pulsars are made of a super-dense solid. This material is so squashed and squeezed that a piece the size of a grain of sand weighs half a million tonnes. An entire pulsar weighs about the same as the Sun, even though it's only 10 kilometres across.

Pulsars are formed when regular stars die. When a star runs out of fuel, it stops shining. The outer layers of the star stop pushing outwards and gravity quickly takes over with a tremendous pulling force. The core then undergoes a catastrophic collapse, creating a massively squashed remnant of the previously mighty star. The tiny particles inside the star, called electrons and protons, get squished so much that they fuse together to create neutrons—that's why pulsars are also known as neutron stars.

As the star gets smaller, it begins to spin faster and faster. Narrow beams of light and radio waves then shoot out of the north and south magnetic poles of the star and shine like a searchlight across our galaxy, waiting to be seen.

Blip—blip—blip! A pulsar is born.

IS THERE LIFE ON OTHER PLANETS?

The oldest evidence of living creatures on this planet comes from tiny fossils in rocks that were found in the Pilbara region of Western Australia. At three-and-a-half billion years of age, these are amongst the oldest rocks in the world. But we are still not completely certain how life on Earth began.

One possibility is that basic life forms originated in outer space, as starlight gave energy to chemicals that were floating around the solar system. These chemicals, which grew bigger as they built up more complex molecules, arrived on Earth billions of years ago via a comet or some rocky, ice-covered body from outer space. Eventually, they may have developed into living creatures, perhaps tiny microbes.

The chemicals may also have fallen onto the Moon, or the other planets in the solar system. The conditions on the host planet would have determined whether or not those chemicals led to complex life.

A second possibility is that the atmosphere on Earth, which billions of years ago was made of methane, ammonia, hydrogen and water vapour, grew its own basic life forms when chemicals in the atmosphere were zapped with energy from lightning storms. This stormy chemical brew may have generated the first microscopic life right here on Earth.

We don't know which of these possibilities is true, but scientists are investigating them to find out. And what of the prospects for life elsewhere in the solar system?

When astronomers looked at the Moon through telescopes more than 400 years ago, they saw mountains and valleys just like the ones on Earth. That was exciting news because no-one had known what the Moon looked like before. Many people started to imagine there could even be life on the Moon.

Then, fifty years ago, we sent spacecraft to the Moon. Some uncrewed spacecraft landed and took pictures and samples of soil, while others had astronauts on board who explored the Moon's surface. We soon discovered that the Moon is a lifeless world, with no atmosphere, and too dry for any living creature to survive.

What if we look further afield to Mars? Is there life there? Again, the answer is no. Humans have sent many robotic spacecraft to Mars, to travel across the surface of the planet taking pictures and collecting soil samples and rocks for scientific study. We have learned from these missions that Mars doesn't host any life at the moment, although it could potentially have been home to basic life forms in the past.

Is there perhaps life on other planets in our solar system?

The other rocky planets, Mercury and Venus, are probably no good for supporting life because their atmospheres are either missing in action (in the case of Mercury) or frazzlingly hot and crushingly thick and acidic (Venus). And the gas giant planets Jupiter, Saturn, Uranus and Neptune are all made of liquid and gas, so we don't know how any life could survive there.

There are also all those moons in our solar system, with some of the most interesting orbiting Jupiter and Saturn. Could they be inhabited? Maybe. But we haven't seen any evidence of life out there.

Of course, it's not just our solar system that we need to consider. There are many other planets out there—LOADS of them! When we look into space with the best telescope we have, we can see thousands of planets around other stars. In fact, around 10 per cent of the stars we have searched have planets around them. And that's just the places we have looked!

If this holds true for the rest of space—that at least 10 per cent of stars have planets—then when we estimate all the stars in the universe, it is likely that there are more than 20 sextillion planets out there. That's 20 000 000 000 000 000 000 000 000 planets!

Do you think that there might be life on one or more of these planets?

A GUIDE TO SPOTTING EXOPLANETS

E ver since we humans began to think about our place in the universe, we have wondered whether there could be other planets out there, orbiting the stars. For centuries we didn't know if there were. But then in 1991, astronomers discovered the very first such planets. It was an amazing discovery because it showed us that our solar system is not unique. There are other worlds out there. We may not even be alone in the universe.

We call them extrasolar planets— 'extrasolar' means outside our solar system—or more commonly, exoplanets. They are very hard to spot because they are so small and extremely far away. Also, they don't shine with their own light but reflect the light from their parent star.

Imagine if Neptune, which is already hard to spot with a telescope, was hundreds of thousands of times further away. That's how difficult it is to find exoplanets. Astronomers have to be very smart to find planets around other stars.

There are a few different ways of doing this. The most successful involves using our old friend gravity.

It is super-difficult to see exoplanets directly. But there's a fantastic way of *indirectly* detecting the presence of these planets, which is to measure the gravitational effect they have on their stars. When a star has one or more planets orbiting around it, the gravitational pull from the planets moves the star ever so slightly from side to side. We call this a wobble, and that's what we're looking for. Our understanding of gravity is so good that we can even measure the size of a planet and its distance from a star using this technique.

Another good way of finding planets around other stars is to wait for a transit. That's where a planet passes in front of the disc of a star, a bit like when the Moon passes in front of the Sun during a solar eclipse. Although the planets are small and only obscure a tiny part of their star, we can still use this method to measure how big a planet is and how far away it is from the star it is orbiting.

Using these methods and a few others, astronomers have found many hundreds of solar systems in our galaxy, containing several thousand planets. The nearest solar system to our own is 40 trillion kilometres away, orbiting the closest star to Earth. The star is called Proxima Centauri and it has at least one planet, called Proxima b.

Rocky, just like the Earth, Proxima b orbits extremely close to its star—eight times closer than Mercury is to the Sun. However,

Proxima Centauri is so dim that its planet only receives a fraction of the light we receive from the Sun. If you lived on Proxima b, the sky would never get brighter than twilight.

Proxima b is likely a bit larger and weighs a little more than the Earth, although we don't know its exact size. But its tiny orbit means that each year only lasts 11.2 Earth days. And we can't tell for sure, but the orbit of Proxima b might be tidally locked, which means that one side of the planet would be in permanent daylight whereas the other side would be constantly dark.

Proxima Centauri is actually part of a triple-star system. The other two stars are Alpha Centauri A and Alpha Centauri B. These appear as a close pair of very bright stars in the sky.

To find out more about this solar system, plans are being developed for a tiny spacecraft capable of travelling at 20 per cent of the speed of light. It would be powered by a huge laser on the Earth, which would push the craft along just like the wind pushes a sailing ship. This spacecraft would take around twenty years to reach Proxima b and could quickly take photos as it whizzed past.

Deeper into space, there are many more complex planetary systems. There are probably 100 billion of them in our Milky Way alone.

As for the big question of whether there is life out there, the answer is that for now, we simply don't know.

SUPERNOVA! WHEN STARS EXPLODE

Imagine that you're looking up at the night sky when suddenly a bright new star appears from nowhere. What would you think?

One thousand years ago, astronomers all around the world—in Asia, Europe and the Middle East—reported just this: a brand new star in the sky. It was brighter than any star they had ever seen. It even shone during the daytime, and some described it as bright as the Moon. But then, after a few months, the star just vanished   it had disappeared as quickly as it had appeared.

So what happened?

We now understand this event to have been a supernova, a catastrophic explosion in which a star destroys itself almost completely at the end of its normal life. The evidence for this is very clear. Instead of the star that once shone there, we can now see a huge spherical region of expanding hot gas. We call this a supernova remnant—the leftovers of the exploded star.

A supernova explosion can happen in a couple of different ways. The first scenario is when a white dwarf star is in orbit with another star.

A white dwarf is an extremely dense core left over from a star like the Sun that has got to the end of its life and pushed most of its gas away. If you grabbed a teaspoon and scooped up some white dwarf material, it would weight more than three cars! When another star orbits a white dwarf, gas from that star gets pulled onto the white dwarf's photosphere—its gassy surface. This slowly increases the amount of gas on the white dwarf, which in turn increases how much it weighs.

White dwarfs can only take so much strain because they are kept in shape by a special force called electron degeneracy pressure— the tiny subatomic particles called electrons don't want to touch one another. When the white dwarf has sucked in enough gas that it weighs 40 per cent more than the Sun, it suddenly collapses. As it gets smaller it becomes unimaginably hot, and at that point the carbon and oxygen in the star ignite. The nuclear fusion of these chemicals releases so much heat that the star suddenly explodes in a colossal supernova.

Another common type of supernova involves a lone star that starts out more than eight times bigger than our Sun. Big stars like this are hot. They burn furiously throughout their short lives, so much so that after a few million years their regular fuel is gone. The hydrogen in the core of the star has all fused into helium. But the temperature in this star is so great that it can also burn helium and carbon and oxygen and more and more chemicals, until the middle of the star is filled with nickel and iron—solid metal!

Once the star is filled with iron, there is nothing left to burn. Its temperature suddenly drops and the star sinks inwards due to the weight of all that gas sitting on top of it. Once the core weighs more than 1.4 times the weight of our Sun, it collapses catastrophically, before bouncing back outwards into space, tearing the star apart.

A supernova is so bright that it can outshine an entire galaxy. If the Sun went supernova, the Earth would boil away until Antarctica was hotter than the surface of our own star. Luckily, our Sun will never, ever go supernova because it's not big or hot enough.

Phew!

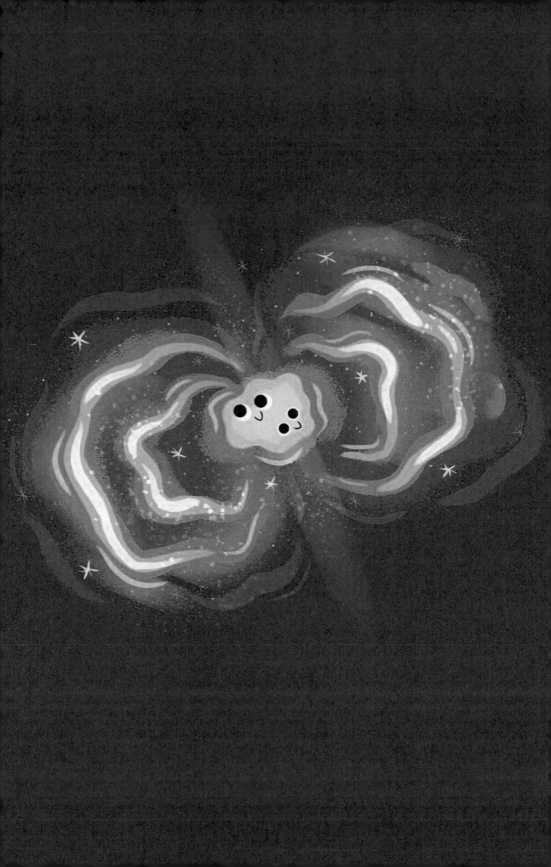

THE BIGGEST STAR IN THE SKY

n a nearby spiral arm of our galaxy, 7500 light-years from Earth, there is a strange object that could be about to blow.

For a long time, Eta Carinae (*ayter ca-riyn-ay*) looked like a pretty ordinary star in the night sky. But in 1837, it suddenly became one of the brightest stars we could see. It continued to increase its illumination for the next five years, gaining an orange hue it had never previously had, before fading and slowly dimming from view. Some fifty years later it brightened again, before dimming once again into obscurity. Over the past sixty years it has yet again brightened gradually to reach naked-eye visibility, and recently there has been some flaring as well.

As we have come to understand more about stars, astronomers have pieced together the reasons for this odd behaviour.

Eta Carinae is not a single star at all. It is a system made up of two stars that live together in a very tight pair. These stars are humungous! One is around 150 times heavier than the Sun, while the other one is around 50 times heavier. These gargantuan stars orbit each other every five-and-a-half years, and together they shine with more than five million times the light of the Sun.

The two stars are so tightly coupled, in fact, that we can't be sure whether or not there are more than two stars. But we do know that whatever is there is behaving extremely strangely and unpredictably.

The first time Eta Carinae got brighter, over 180 years ago, this event was called 'the great eruption'. We are now able to study exactly what happened during this explosion. The light from it reflected off nearby interstellar clouds of gas and bounced back in our direction, finally reaching the Earth in the last few years. We call these signals 'light echoes', and what they show us is that during the eruption, gas and dust streamed off the stars at an unimaginably fast speed of 32 million kilometres per hour. That's faster than a supernova, when a star reaches the end of its normal life and explodes.

The eruption was probably caused by a third star orbiting with the system being ripped apart and sucked onto the surface of the remaining stars. When hot gas from one star falls onto another, there is a huge explosion of energy and light. Vast quantities of gas and dust particles are released. We can still see this gas and dust, which has settled around Eta Carinae as an amazing nebula—it's as if someone has captured a picture of the explosion and it is still going on today.

The dust in this nebula is what caused the change in colour and fading of the starlight after Eta Carinae had its major eruption. Later eruptions were smaller and more short-lived.

The interesting question now is: What will happen next?

It is possible that, sometime in the next few million years, at least one of the stars that make up Eta Carinae will explode as a supernova. If this were to happen, Eta Carinae could shine brighter than any other star. And if it erupted in a catastrophic explosion called a hypernova, it could shine as brightly as the Moon. Alternatively, either of the giant stars could collapse without first going supernova, forming a black hole.

Regardless, the likelihood of a supernova involving one of these massive stars is very strong. The question really is not if, but when.

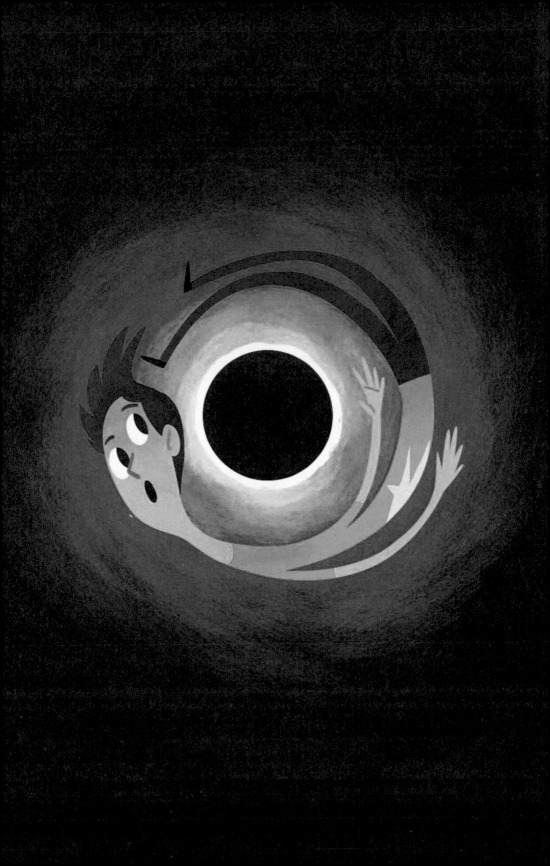

HOW DOES A STAR BECOME A BLACK HOLE?

lack holes are amazing! They might sound like science fiction but they're very real. We scientists have weighed them, watched them collide, and taken pictures of them ripping up and devouring stars. There is no doubt at all that black holes exist.

Some black holes were made at the centres of galaxies when the universe was quite young. As a gigantic blob of gas was pulled together by the force of gravity, a galaxy formed. In the middle of the galaxy, part of this gas became a supermassive black hole, more than a million times heavier than the Sun. The trouble is, we don't yet know for sure how this happened.

Many black holes, though, are stars that have got to the end of their lives and turned themselves inside out. Now, instead of shining outwards, they suck light back in due to their enormous gravitational pull. And this is something we do understand.

So how does a star become a black hole?

Stars come in lots of different sizes. The Sun is a rather small, cool star. We call it a yellow dwarf. Its surface layer is only 6000 degrees Celsius—that's still pretty hot though, so don't touch! The biggest stars are much hotter than the Sun, and they also burn hundreds of thousands of times brighter. The hottest star ever discovered, called WR102, has a temperature of 200 000 degrees Celsius on its surface. Pretty steamy, hey?

Hot stars like WR102 shine exceedingly bright and burn their fuel incredibly quickly. This fuel is the gas that lies deep in the core of the star. Once that gas has run out, the star stops shining. At that point, gravity takes over and pulls the star inwards very quickly. Everything in the star collapses into the middle.

If the star is REALLY big—more than ten times the size of the Sun—the gas will bounce back and explode in a gigantic cosmic fireball called a supernova. If the star is EXTREMELY big—weighing more than twenty times our Sun—gravity will be strong enough to keep pulling it together forever. The star will get smaller and smaller and smaller, sucking all the gas, particles and even light into a tiny point, smaller than the tip of a pencil.

This is a black hole. It is the relic of a gigantic, bright star that lived a long and happy life before curling up into a ball.

Like any object in space, black holes have a gravitational pull. And because they are very heavy, their gravitational pull on nearby objects is quite strong. If a star gets too close to a black hole, gravity will pull it into an orbit. The star will then steadily circle the black hole, just like the Earth circles the Sun. Imagine having a black hole for a sun.

Some stars are unlucky and get way too close. Gravity will slowly stretch these stars like pasta—we call this spaghettification!—and eventually rip them apart. When a star is destroyed like this, its guts are ripped out and its gassy remains fall into the black hole.

We can sometimes see this process happening. In galaxies that have supermassive black holes at their centres, we can see a ring of extremely hot gas that is orbiting around the black hole. This gas has a temperature in excess of a billion degrees Celsius. As the gas circles round, faster and faster, it shines brightly before it falls over the edge of the black hole, never to be seen again.

As black holes feed on stars, they get heavier and more powerful. At some point, there will be no stars or planets left at all. The whole universe will be filled with black holes.

But that won't happen for a very long time, perhaps trillions of years.

PART 4
THE MILKY WAY

OUR GALAXY—COUNTLESS STARS

I f you go somewhere really dark at night, away from streetlights and houses and cars and people, you might see something very special in the sky. It's a band of light that stretches far overhead, from one horizon to the other. We call it the Milky Way.

For tens of thousands of years, people have looked at the Milky Way and wondered what makes this incredible glowing pathway across the sky. Some people used to think it was a river of milk cascading through the heavens, which is how it got its name. Others believed it was a river reflecting the moonlight, or a flock of geese flying through the sky.

Since the invention of the telescope, we have discovered that the Milky Way is actually made up of countless stars that are so far away their lights blur together.

The Milky Way is our galaxy, our home—a vast cosmic city where the Sun is only one of more than 200 billion stars. It not only contains a huge number of stars but thousands of millions of planets too. At its centre is a supermassive black hole that is wider than our solar system and contains more than 4 million Suns' worth of gas. That colossal black hole is slowly eating stars today.

The Milky Way is spinning around, which means it has flattened into a disc, like a pizza. Because it is shaped like this, it looks like a thin line of light across the sky. Within this disc is an amazing spiral shape, like a curled-up space centipede or an interstellar octopus. We live inside this spiral, along with the Sun, all the planets of our solar system, and every single star we can see.

Our cosmic city is truly enormous. If you travelled at the fastest possible speed—the speed of light—for 100000 years, you would still not reach the other side of the galaxy. That's how big the Milky Way really is.

Our galaxy is not alone in space. Because of its gigantic gravitational field, the Milky Way has a swarm of fifty or so mini-galaxies orbiting it, like a galaxy family. Two of these galaxies can easily be seen in the night sky, if you're in a dark place. They are called the Magellanic (*madge-el-lanik*) clouds. Although they look like cloudy patches of light in the night sky, each one is a collection of literally millions of stars—an entire galaxy in its own right.

Our galaxy is also connected to two larger spiral galaxies by mutual gravitational attraction. These are called the Andromeda galaxy and the Triangulum galaxy.

The Milky Way won't last forever. In about four billion years we will collide with our neighbours in the spiral, causing amazing fireworks and changing the face of our galaxy. But for now, you can check it out when you're somewhere dark.

It's the greatest show on Earth.

SUPERMASSIVE–VISITING A BLACK HOLE

The year is 2045. You're about to go on an historic mission—to execute the first ever fly-by of a supermassive black hole. Destination, Sagittarius. The centre of the Milky Way.

For this daring adventure, a special light-drive has been developed by the International Space Agency. It should enable your spacecraft to travel close to the speed of light on this unprecedented excursion to the heart of our galaxy. You, as the first galactic astronaut, will be testing this new system. You understand that this is a very dangerous journey, and that you won't be returning to Earth as you know it.

As the spacecraft zooms away from Earth, you stay alert. Soon you must trigger scientific observations of the solar system. The window of opportunity for these activities is small. You reach Mars in a little over four minutes, the stripy gas giant Jupiter in thirty-five minutes, and after another half-hour, the ringed planet Saturn. Within five hours, the entire solar system is behind you.

Your mission plan is clear about what comes next. The nearest star will not appear for another four years, so you settle down in the cryogenic unit and prepare for a deep sleep. Since your destination is 25 643 light-years away, you set your alarm for the year 27 688.

After what seems like no time at all, you wake up, groggy and thirsty from your sleep. It felt like the blink of an eye, but you know that more than 25 000 years have passed. You think with sadness about what you left behind. Everyone you knew on Earth is now gone. You have permanently swapped your familiar environment for this strange new one.

Wanting to clear your head and get your bearings, you grab a glass of water and go down to the stellar observation deck. Here, the reinforced glass windows give you an amazing 180-degree vista of deep space.

The first thing you notice are the hundreds of brilliant blue stars that stand out against a perfectly black sky. There are no familiar constellations, though, like the ones you used to see from your backyard on Earth. These stars are ones you've never seen before.

As you zoom towards your destination, a cloud of black dust gathers ahead, slowly thickening as you approach and blotting out more and more stars. Suddenly, you punch into this cloud and are enveloped by it. You see fewer stars now, but the ones you do see are in bright and brilliant clusters, shining blue and white.

The countdown timer for your destination hits sixty seconds. The automatic braking system engages, jolting you. As the spacecraft slows down, you're pulled forward in your seat.

That's when you see it. A fuzzy, glowing arc of light comes into focus, squashed like a flying saucer from an old science fiction movie. In the centre is a disc of complete darkness and surrounding this is a perfect circle of light—a swirling ring of hot gas that has been bent by a tremendous gravitational field.

This is it, you say to yourself. This is the supermassive black hole.

Steady with the controls. Don't get too close. If you do, you know that your spacecraft could be pulled into an orbit filled with searing hot gas, in excess of 1 billion degrees Celsius. Or worse still, into a collision course with the black hole itself.

You back off the throttle a little and take in this magnificent sight.

Incredible. A black hole. Something that no human eyes have ever before seen up close.

TRAVELLING AT THE SPEED OF LIGHT

You might have heard the phrase 'travelling at the speed of light'. The speed of light is unimaginably quick. It's faster than a speeding bullet, swifter than a bird in flight, speedier than a rocket on its way to the Moon. In fact, light is so fast that it travels eight times around the Earth in a single second!

The speed of light is faster than everything. It's the fastest speed there is. Three hundred thousand kilometres per second.

We don't normally use kilometres as a measure of distances in space, though. Because kilometres are so small, and the universe is so big, we measure distances in terms of how long it takes light to travel between two places. For example, sunlight bouncing off the Moon takes 1.3 seconds to reach the Earth, so we say that the Moon is 1.3 light-seconds from Earth. This also means that all communications with astronauts on the Moon are delayed by that amount of time, since nothing—not even an astronaut's radio transmissions—can travel faster than light.

Light from the Sun takes eight minutes to reach our eyes here on Earth. (If the Sun was suddenly switched off, we wouldn't know about it for at least eight minutes!) That means that the Sun and the Earth are eight light-minutes apart—that's 150 million kilometres.

Moving out beyond our solar system, the light shining from the nearest star, Proxima Centauri, takes 4.2 years to zoom through space and reach the Earth. Proxima Centauri is said to be 4.2 light-years away.

This raises problems with interstellar travel. Imagine if we sent astronauts to visit Proxima Centauri and explore its Earth-like planet, Proxima b. Every time the people at mission control wanted to speak to the astronauts, the message would take 4.2 years to reach them. When the astronauts replied, it would take another 4.2 years for their message to return to Earth. This would make conversations very difficult.

Going out further still, a beam of light takes 2.5 million years to travel from the nearest spiral galaxy—the Andromeda galaxy—to the Earth. That means the light that is reaching us from the Andromeda galaxy today left that galaxy before human beings had evolved from our ape-like ancestors.

When we look this far into space, we are literally looking back in time.

More distant galaxies give us an even deeper insight into the past. Using hugely powerful telescopes, we can see the nearest quasar, an extra-bright galaxy 600 million light-years away. The light that has just shone to us from that quasar left on its cosmic journey before the dinosaurs roamed the Earth. That means we can tell what such galaxies were like millions of years ago.

You could say that a telescope is a time machine. By showing us objects so far away, it allows us to study what stars and galaxies used to be like millions of years ago, and to figure out the history of our universe.

Isn't that mind-blowing?

WHY DO QUASARS SHINE SO BRIGHT?

Far away in the depths of space lurks a breed of galaxy so strange and so powerful that it was given a very special name—quasar (*kway-zar*). Along with 'black hole', the word 'quasar' has got to be the most futuristic, spacey name there is!

Quasars were noticed when astronomers started using radio telescopes in the 1940s. Unlike the optical telescopes we look through with our eyes, these telescopes look at radio waves coming from outer space. Radio waves are just like light waves, but are a very different colour. We can't see them with our eyes because they have a very long wavelength and won't fit in our eyeballs.

When quasars were first spotted, no-one knew what they were. Through a regular telescope, they just looked like faint starry-type things, with nothing much to distinguish them from ordinary stars. Some were even completely invisible to normal telescopes. But when astronomers looked at them using a radio telescope, they were the brightest things in the sky. These mysterious objects were called 'quasi-stellar radio sources', or quasars for short.

Quasar light was different to that of a normal star, and it soon became clear that they were extremely far away from the Earth. They were also extraordinarily small for objects so bright. Astronomers scratched their heads, unable to figure out how something so small and so far away could shine so brightly. It turned out that quasars are so bright because they lie at the heart of galaxies that have supermassive black holes.

When a star gets too close to a black hole at the centre of a galaxy, it gradually gets pulled even closer under the influence of gravity. Near the edge of the black hole, the gravitational forces become extremely strong. At this point, the star stretches and is completely ripped apart. When this happens, the searing hot gas from the destroyed star spins around and around the black hole extremely quickly. The friction from this hot disc of gas creates a spectacular cauldron of heat, light and energy.

This is a quasar. It is the colossal fireworks sparking at the centre of a galaxy, as if screaming, 'Hey! There's a black hole here and it's eating stars!'

Quasars shine 100 times brighter than the Milky Way, and we can see them right across the length and breadth of our universe. One of the most distant objects ever seen is a quasar that lies more than 13.1 billion light-years away from Earth.

The black holes that power quasars devour 1000 Suns per year. Some are so powerful that they blow energetic fountains of bright gas out into space at close to the speed of light. No wonder some people call quasars 'the dragons of the night sky'.

THE BIG BANG THEORY

The Big Bang was the beginning of our universe.

Around 13.8 billion years ago, everything that exists—all of space and time—was crammed together into a single point. We call this a singularity. The Big Bang was the event when this tiny point containing all the energy and all the material in the universe began to expand. It grew incredibly quickly, cooling as it got bigger.

A fraction of a second after the Big Bang, subatomic particles were released, including matter and antimatter. One second after the Big Bang, the universe, which continued to expand, was filled with tiny particles like electrons, protons and neutrons, and its temperature was 5.5 billion degrees Celsius.

A few minutes after the Big Bang, the universe had cooled down a bit from this unbearable inferno, but it was still as hot as the burning core of a star. Neutrons and protons joined together as they collided, just like the nuclear fusion inside a star.

After about twenty minutes, the universe had expanded so much that conditions were no longer so ferociously hot. It had cooled down enough to stop nuclear fusion. But it was still too hot for whole atoms to exist. Atoms have a middle, called the nucleus, which is made up of protons and neutrons. They also have a cloud of electrons whizzing around them. When it's very hot, the electrons get too excited and have too much energy. Because they're so fidgety, they can't stay close to the nucleus to make up whole atoms.

In that initial period after the Big Bang, all the electrons whirled around in space like a fiery swarm of insects. Light couldn't travel more than a short distance before it bounced off a tiny particle, so nothing was visible at that time except a dense fog. But as the universe ballooned further, it cooled more and more. Around 380 000 years after the Big Bang, the universe was finally cool enough to allow atoms to form.

At last—atoms are what make up our bodies and everything on Earth!

We have managed to take a photo of the universe from this time, when it was a baby. It's called the cosmic microwave background and it's an image that was taken using special cameras mounted on radio telescopes.

The picture was created by looking at invisible microwaves, like the ones we use inside microwave ovens to heat up food. We can actually 'see' these microwaves from outer space, which have travelled from the early cosmic gas towards our telescopes for billions of years, since the early times of the universe. That's why we can take a picture of something that happened before the Earth even existed. Amazing!

The cosmic microwave background shows that when the universe was very young, it was hot and looked almost exactly the same in all directions. It would have been a pretty boring place to live in. But as the universe expanded further, it cooled down a lot. Atoms weren't whizzing around like flies anymore, and gas began to settle down into clouds that floated calmly in space. After a few hundred million years, the first stars and galaxies began to form, shaped and moulded by gravity.

As the expansion of space continued, more and more galaxies appeared. Shepherded by the mysterious substance we call 'dark matter', which is completely invisible but has a strong gravitational pull on stars and galaxies, gravity formed these galaxies into giant families that we call galaxy clusters. These clusters are still around today—in fact, we live inside one of them.

Today, the universe is still expanding. New galaxies are still forming, growing and merging. The universe is a startling living project. I think we're lucky to be part of it.

SURFING GRAVITATIONAL WAVES

Splish splash! Have you ever spun around in a swimming pool and made waves? Maybe you've darted and twirled around, causing ripples that bounce and cascade towards the pool's edge.

Well, have you ever imagined there could be waves like that in the air? There are. As you clap your hands or stomp your feet, waves of sound move out in all directions. These are invisible to our eyes but not to our ears.

Are there other waves you cannot see? Again, yes. Think about the tectonic plates shifting and jolting underground and beneath the seas. Consider the earthquakes that rumble and grumble through the ground, maybe shaking and rattling your own house.

And what about in space? What waves are out there?

Imagine stars and black holes twisting and colliding in faraway places. And planets stomping and splashing their way through space. These all send ripples across the universe.

We are constantly surfing the waves caused by the constant motion of trillions of stars, and other cosmic bodies. We are floating in a sea of gravitational waves.

HOW BIG IS THE UNIVERSE?

The universe is everything. All the stars, all the planets, all the rocky bits like comets and asteroids, every galaxy, every black hole, and all the space in-between. The universe is bigger than any of us can imagine.

The Earth is 12 756 kilometres across. It takes about two days to fly around the world in an aeroplane. The object nearest to us in space is the Moon, around 380 000 kilometres away. It takes two days to fly to the Moon in the fastest spacecraft we have. After that, we stop measuring in kilometres because the distances become too great. In space, we measure distances in light-years, or how long it takes light to travel between two places.

The speed of light is 300 000 kilometres every second. Whoosh! That's so fast that a beam of light zips around the world at a rate of seven times every second.

Our solar system is seventeen light-hours across. That means it takes a beam of light seventeen hours to zoom from the Sun to the edge of the solar system. That's 18.8 billion kilometres.

The Milky Way galaxy is MUCH bigger. It contains all the stars we can see in the sky, which are all spaced out with several light-years between each one. The Milky Way is a whopping 100 000 light years across. That's too big to even imagine!

But that's not all. There are trillions of galaxies in the universe, each separated from the others by unimaginable distances of nearly empty space.

So how big *is* the whole universe? That's a very difficult question to answer. We can't just get a ruler out and measure the universe. We can't travel across the universe and see how big it is.

And to make it even harder, the universe is getting bigger and bigger every day. When we look into space, we see that the galaxies are getting further and further apart, and that is because the universe is expanding. It's not just expanding now. It has been expanding for 13.8 billion years, ever since the Big Bang.

The Big Bang was the time when everything that exists was crammed into a tiny space that was infinitely small. Smaller than a full stop. Smaller than an atom! For reasons that we don't yet understand, everything suddenly rushed apart.

The universe keeps expanding to this day, like a balloon that's always being blown up. In fact, the universe is expanding faster today than it was yesterday, which suggests that it will continue expanding forever.

The universe is bigger than we can ever see.

We see things in other parts of the universe because they give off light, and that light travels all the way across outer space and eventually goes into our eyeballs (or telescopes). Light travels at 300 000 kilometres per second, but it still takes a REALLY long time for it to reach us from distant galaxies, because they are so far away. So long in fact, that the light from some galaxies has taken billions of years to reach us.

This sets a limit on how far we can see. If an object is very far away, we will never, ever see it. Because the distance to faraway galaxies is getting bigger, the light from them will keep travelling towards us but NEVER, EVER reach us.

The universe that we can see includes all the galaxies that are visible. That area stretches for 13.8 billion light-years in every direction. But as the universe has expanded since the light began its journey, that area is now 93 billion light years across. Mind-bending or what?

We can't know the size of the WHOLE universe for sure. It is possible that it has a limited size, estimated by some scientists as seven trillion light-years! But it is also possible that the universe is infinite—it goes on forever. That idea is so hard for you and me to imagine.

Boom! Splat! That was my mind exploding.

FURTHER EXPLORING

- Information about the International Space Station (including a virtual tour): https://www.nasa.gov/mission_pages/station/main/index.html
- Amazing images of stars, planets, galaxies, nebulae, comets and asteroids from the Hubble Space Telescope: http://hubblesite.org
- Recommended night sky apps for smartphones or tablets (download from wherever you get your apps):
  Sky Guide ($4.49)—Includes an amazing augmented-reality view of the night sky and the positions of satellites. You can set up alerts for interesting events, including International Space Station flyovers, meteor showers and planetary conjunctions. Well worth the price.
  SkyView Lite (free)—A good, basic app for locating stars and planets.
- Monthly sky guides from Sydney Observatory: https://maas.museum/observations/category/monthly-sky-guides
- Local astronomical societies in Australia and New Zealand: https://spaceinfo.com.au/links/clubs-societies

ACKNOWLEDGEMENTS

For planting the seeds of *Under the Stars: Astrophysics for Everyone*, I would like to thank Shell Reid, Sally Heath and Emma Rusher. As always, I am grateful to the entire team at Melbourne University Publishing for their diligent and professional work. Thanks to my parents, who created the rich and fertile learning environment that enabled my brain to consider the world beyond the clouds. And finally, I am eternally grateful to all the incredible young people around the world who ask the bamboozling questions that encourage me to continue exploring the universe.

Lisa Harvey-Smith is an award-winning astronomer and a professor at the University of New South Wales. In 2018 she was appointed as the Australian Government's Ambassador for Women in Science, Technology, Engineering and Mathematics (STEM). Lisa uses the world's most powerful telescopes to study the birth and death of stars and the properties of supermassive black holes.

Lisa is a regular on television and radio and is a presenter on the ABC's hit TV show *Stargazing Live*. She has toured the nation with her live shows 'When Galaxies Collide' and has previously hosted live stage shows with Apollo astronauts including Buzz Aldrin, Gene Cernan and Charlie Duke.

To get away from it all, Lisa enjoys ultra-marathon and multi-day races. She once ran 250 kilometres across the Simpson Desert.

Mel Matthews is an illustrator who lives and works on the beautiful Mornington Peninsula in Victoria. After a brief stint as a jazz musician, she studied fine art and illustration before becoming a full-time illustrator, creating artwork for books, games and products of all kinds. When she's not drawing, Mel can usually be found swimming, reading, writing, talking to parrots, or looking for the ISS on a clear starry night.